Dewey

Dewey

The Small–Town Library Cat Who Touched the World

VICKI MYRON
with BRET WITTER

HODDER

First published in Great Britain in 2009 by Hodder & Stoughton
An Hachette Livre UK company

First published in paperback in 2009

1

Grateful acknowledgment is given to W.P. Kinsella for
permission to quote in Chapter 14 from *Shoeless Joe* by
W.P. Kinsella (Boston: Houghton Mifflin, 1982)

A CIP catalogue record for this title is
available from the British Library

ISBN 978 0 340 95395 2

Typeset by Hewer Text UK Ltd, Edinburgh
Printed and bound in the UK by CPI Mackays, Chatham ME5 8TD

Hodder & Stoughton policy is to use papers that are
natural, renewable and recyclable products and made
from wood grown in sustainable forests. The logging and
manufacturing processes are expected to conform to the
environmental regulations of the country of origin.

Hodder & Stoughton Ltd
338 Euston Road
London NW1 3BH

www.hodder.co.uk

To Gran, Mom, and Jodi –
three amazing women who loved
Dewey almost as much as I do

Contents

INTRODUCTION

Welcome to Iowa

There is a thousand-mile table of land in the middle of the United States, between the Mississippi River on the east and the deserts on the west. Out here, there are rolling hills, but no mountains. There are rivers and creeks, but few large lakes. The wind has worn down the rock outcroppings, turning them first to dust, then dirt, then soil, and finally to fine black farmland. Out here, the roads are straight, stretching to the horizon in long, unbroken lines. There are no corners, only occasional, almost imperceptible bends. This land was surveyed and plotted for farms; the bends are corrections in the survey line. Exactly every mile, every road is intersected by another almost perfectly straight road. Inside is a square mile of farmland. Take a million of those square miles, lace them together, and you have one of the most important agricultural regions in the world. The Great Plains. The Bread Basket. The Heartland. Or, as many people think of it, the place you fly over on your way to somewhere else. Let them have the oceans and mountains, their beaches and their ski resorts. I'll take Iowa.

In northwest Iowa, in winter, the sky swallows the

farmhouses. On a cold day, the dark clouds that blow
in across the plains seem to churn the land under like
a plow. In the spring, the world is flat and empty, full
of brown dirt and hacked-off cornstalks waiting to be
plowed under, the sky and land perfectly balanced
like a plate on a stick. But if you come in the late
summer, you would swear the ground is about to
push up and tip the sky right out of the picture. The
corn is nine feet high, bright green leaves topped with
brilliant gold tassels. Most of the time you are buried
in it, lost in the walls of corn, but top a small rise
in the road, just a few feet of elevation, and you can
see endless fields of gold atop green, silken threads
sparkling in the sun. Those silks are the sex organs of
the corn, trapping pollen, flying golden yellow for a
month and then slowly drying up and browning out
under the stiff summer heat.

That's what I love about northwest Iowa: it is
always changing. Not in the way the suburbs change
as one chain restaurant replaces another or the way
cities change as buildings crowd each other ever
higher, but in the way the country changes, slowly
back and forth in a gentle motion that is always sliding
forward, but never very fast. There aren't many
roadside businesses out here. No crafts stores. No
farmers' markets. The farmhouses, which are fewer
every year, hug the road. The towns pop up suddenly,
bearing signs announcing THE JEWEL IN THE CROWN
OF IOWA or THE GOLD BUCKLE ON THE CORN BELT, and
disappear just as quickly. Two minutes, and they're

gone. A grain elevator or a processing plant, maybe a downtown strip with a convenience store, a place to eat. Every ten miles or so, there's a roadside cemetery, small plain markers behind low stone walls. These are pioneer plots that grew into extended family plots and eventually into town cemeteries. Nobody wants to be buried far from home, and nobody wants to waste much land. Use what you have. Make it simple. Keep it local.

Then, just when you're sliding away, when you're drifting into complacency like a corn row down the back side of a rise, the road widens and you pass a strip of stores: Matt Furniture, the Iron Horse Hotel, the Prime Rib restaurant, but also a Wal-Mart, a McDonald's, a Motel 6. Turn north at the stoplight, the first turn in fifty miles no matter which direction you've been driving, not to mention the first stoplight, and within a minute you've left the chains behind and you're driving the beautiful low bridge over the Little Sioux River right into the heart of Spencer, Iowa, a town that hasn't changed much since 1931.

Downtown Spencer is picture postcard small-town America: rows of storefronts in connecting two-and-three-story buildings where people pull their cars to the curb, get out, and walk. White Drug, Eddie Quinn's Men's Clothing, and Steffen Furniture have been in business for decades. The Hen House sells decorating items to farmwives and the occasional tourist on her way to the Iowa lake country twenty miles north. There's a hobby shop specializing in model airplanes, a card shop, and a store that rents oxygen tanks and wheelchairs. The Vacuum Cleaner Store. Arts on Grand. The old movie theater is still in business, although it shows only second-run movies since a seven-screen cineplex opened south of the bridge.

The downtown ends at The Hotel, eight blocks from the bridge. The Hotel. That's the actual name. It was known as the Tagney in the late 1920s when it was the area's best accommodation, bus depot, train station, and only sit-down restaurant. By the end of the Great Depression, it had become a flophouse and, according to legend, the town bordello. The five-story building, plain redbrick and built to last, was eventually abandoned, then rehabilitated in the 1970s, but by then the real action had moved five blocks down Grand Avenue to Sister's Main Street Café, a no-frills diner with Formica tables, drip coffee, and smoky booths. Three groups of men congregate every morning at Sister's: the old guys, the older guys, and the really old guys. Together, they have run Spencer for the past sixty years.

Around the corner from Sister's Café, across a small parking lot and just half a block off Grand Avenue, is a low gray concrete building: the Spencer Public Library. My name is Vicki Myron, and I've been working in that library for twenty-five years, the last twenty as director. I've overseen the arrival of the first computer and the addition of the reading room. I've watched children grow up and leave, only to walk back through the doors ten years later with their own children. The Spencer Public Library may not look like much, at least not at first, but it is the centerpiece, the middle ground, the heart of this heartland story. Everything I'm going to tell you about Spencer – and about the surrounding farms, the nearby lakes, the Catholic church in Hartley, the Moneta School, the box factory, and the wonderful old white Ferris wheel up at Arnold's Park – all flows back eventually to this small gray building and to the cat who lived here for more than nineteen years.

How much of an impact can an animal have? How many lives can one cat touch? How is it possible for an abandoned kitten to transform a small library into a meeting place and tourist attraction, inspire a classic American town, bind together an entire region, and eventually become famous around the world? You can't even begin to answer those questions until you hear the story of Dewey Readmore Books, the beloved library cat of Spencer, Iowa.

I

The Coldest Morning

January 18, 1988, was a bitterly cold Iowa Monday. The night before, the temperature had reached minus fifteen degrees, and that didn't take into account the wind, which cut under your coat and squeezed your bones. It was a killing freeze, the kind that made it almost painful to breathe. The problem with flat land, as all of Iowa knows, is that there's nothing to stop the weather. It blows out of Canada, across the Dakotas, and straight into town. The first bridge in Spencer across the Little Sioux, built in the late 1800s, had to be taken down because the river became so jammed with ice everyone worried the pylons would collapse. When the town water tower burned down in 1893 – the straw packing used to keep the riser pipe from freezing caught fire, and all the nearby fire hydrants were frozen solid – a two-foot-thick, ten-foot-wide circle of ice slid out the top of the tank, crushed the community recreation center, and shattered all over Grand Avenue. That's winter in Spencer for you.

I have never been a morning person, especially on a dark and cloudy January day, but I have always been dedicated. There were a few cars on the road at seven thirty, when I drove the ten blocks to work, but as usual mine was the first car in the parking lot. Across the street, the Spencer Public Library was dead – no lights, no movement, no sound until I flipped a switch and brought it to life. The heater switched on automatically during the night, but the library was still a freezer first thing in the morning. Whose idea was it to build a concrete and glass building in northern Iowa? I needed my coffee.

I went immediately to the library staff room – nothing more than a kitchenette with a microwave and a sink, a refrigerator too messy for most people's taste, a few chairs, and a phone for personal calls – hung up my coat, and started the coffee. Then I scanned the Saturday newspaper. Most local issues could affect, or could be affected by, the library. The local newspaper, the *Spencer Daily Reporter*, didn't publish on Sunday or Monday, so Monday was catch-up morning for the Saturday edition.

'Good morning, Vicki,' said Jean Hollis Clark, the assistant library director, taking off her scarf and mittens. 'It's a mean one out there.'

'Good morning, Jean,' I said, putting aside the paper.

In the center of the staff room, against the back wall, was a large metal box with a hinged lid. The box was two feet high and four feet square, about the size of a two-person kitchen table if you sawed the legs in half. A metal chute rose out of the top of the box, then disappeared into the wall. At the other end, in the alley behind the building, was a metal slot: the library's after-hours book return.

You find all kinds of things in a library drop box – garbage, rocks, snowballs, soda cans. Librarians don't talk about it, because it gives people ideas, but all libraries deal with it. Video stores probably have the same problem. Stick a slot in a wall and you're asking for trouble, especially if, as it did at the Spencer Public Library, the slot opened onto a back alley across the street from the town's middle school. Several times we had been startled in the middle of the afternoon by a loud pop from the drop box. Inside, we'd find a firecracker.

After the weekend, the drop box would also be full of books, so every Monday I loaded them onto one of our book carts so the clerks could process and shelve them later in the day. When I came back with the cart on this particular Monday morning, Jean was standing quietly in the middle of the room.

'I heard a noise.'

'What kind of noise?'

'From the drop box. I think it's an animal.'

'A what?'

'An animal. I think there's an animal in the drop box.'

That was when I heard it, a low rumble from under the metal cover. It didn't sound like an animal. It sounded more like an old man struggling to clear his throat. But I doubted it was an old man. The opening at the top of the chute was only a few inches wide, so that would be quite a squeeze. It was an animal, I had little doubt of that, but what kind? I got down on my knees, reached over to the lid, and hoped for a chipmunk.

The first thing I felt was a blast of freezing air. Someone had jammed a book into the return slot, wedging it open. It was as cold in the box as it was outside; maybe colder, since the box was lined with metal. You could have kept frozen meat in there. I was still catching my breath when I saw the kitten.

It was huddled in the front left corner of the box, its head down, its legs tucked underneath it, trying to appear as small as possible. The books were piled haphazardly to the top of the box, partially hiding it from view. I lifted one gingerly for a better look. The kitten looked up at me, slowly and sadly. Then it lowered its head and sank down into its hole. It wasn't trying to appear tough. It wasn't trying to hide. I don't even think it was scared. It was just hoping to be saved.

I know melting can be a cliché, but I think that's what actually happened to me at that moment: I lost every bone in my body. I am not a mushy person. I'm a single mother and a farm girl who has steered her life through hard times, but this was so, so . . . unexpected.

I lifted the kitten out of the box. My hands nearly swallowed it. We found out later it was eight weeks old, but it looked no more than eight days old, if that. It was so thin I could see every rib. I could feel its heart beating, its lungs pumping. The poor kitten was so weak it could barely hold up its head, and it was shaking uncontrollably. It opened its mouth, but the sound, which came two seconds later, was weak and ragged.

And cold. That's what I remember most, because I couldn't believe a living animal could be so cold. It felt like there was no warmth at all. So I cradled the kitten in my arms to share my heat. It didn't fight. Instead, it snuggled into my chest, then laid its head against my heart.

'Oh, my golly,' said Jean.

'The poor baby,' I said, squeezing tighter.

'It's adorable.'

Neither of us said anything for a while. We were just staring at the kitten. Finally Jean said, 'How do you think it got in there?'

I wasn't thinking about last night. I was only thinking about right now. It was too early to call the veterinarian, who wouldn't be in for an hour. But the kitten was so cold. Even in the warmth of my arms, I could feel it shaking.

'We've got to do something,' I said.

Jean grabbed a towel, and we wrapped the little fellow up until only its nose was sticking out, its huge eyes staring from the shadows in disbelief.

'Let's give it a warm bath,' I said. 'Maybe that will stop the shivering.'

I filled the staff room sink with warm water, testing it with my elbow as I clutched the kitten in my arms.

It slid into the sink like a block of ice. Jean found some shampoo in the art closet, and I rubbed the kitten slowly and lovingly, almost petting it. As the water turned grayer and grayer, the kitten's wild shivering turned to soft purring. I smiled. This kitten was tough. But it was so very young. When I finally lifted it out of the sink, it looked like a newborn: huge lidded eyes and big ears sticking out from a tiny head and an even smaller body. Wet, defenseless, and meowing quietly for its mother.

We dried it with the blow dryer we used for drying glue at craft time. Within thirty seconds, I was holding a beautiful, long-haired orange tabby. The kitten had been so filthy, I had thought it was gray.

By this time Doris and Kim had arrived, and there were four people in the staff room, each cooing over the kitten. Eight hands touched it, seemingly at once. The other three staffers talked over one another while I stood silently cradling the kitten like a baby and rocking back and forth from foot to foot.

'Where did it come from?'

'The drop box.'

'No!'

'Is it a boy or a girl?'

I glanced up. They were all looking at me. 'A boy,' I said.

'He's beautiful.'

'How old is he?'

'How did he get in the box?'

I wasn't listening. I only had eyes for the kitten.

'It's so cold.'

'Bitterly cold.'

'The coldest morning of the year.'

A pause, then: 'Someone must have put him in the box.'

'That's awful.'

'Maybe they were trying to save him. From the cold.'

'I don't know . . . he's so helpless.'

'He's so young.'

'He's so beautiful. Oh, he's breaking my heart.'

I put him down on the table. The poor kitten could barely stand. The pads on all four of his paws were frostbitten, and over the next week they would turn white and peel off. And yet the kitten managed to do something truly amazing. He steadied himself on the table and slowly looked up into each face. Then he began to hobble. As each person reached to pet him, he rubbed his tiny head against her hand and purred. Forget the horrible events in his young life. Forget the cruel person who shoved him down that library drop box. It was as if, from that moment on, he wanted to personally thank every person he ever met for saving his life.

By now it had been twenty minutes since I pulled the kitten out of the drop box, and I'd had plenty of time to think through a few things – the once common practice of keeping library cats, my ongoing plan to make the library more friendly and appealing, the logistics of bowls and food and cat litter, the trusting expression on the kitten's face when he burrowed into my chest and looked up into my eyes. So I was more than prepared when someone finally asked, 'What should we do with him?'

'Well,' I said, as if the thought had just occurred to me, 'maybe we can keep him.'

2

A Perfect Addition

The most amazing thing about the kitten was how happy he was that first day. Here he was in a new environment, surrounded by eager strangers who wanted nothing more than to squeeze him, fondle him, and coo over him, and he was perfectly calm. No matter how many times we passed him from hand to hand, and no matter what position we held him in, he was never jumpy or fidgety. He never tried to bite or get away. Instead, he just melted into each person's arms and stared up into her eyes.

And that was no small feat, because we didn't leave him alone for a second. If someone had to set him down – for instance, because there was actual work to do – there were always at least five sets of hands ready to grab him, hold him, and love him. In fact, when I set him down at closing time that first night, I had to watch him for five minutes to make sure he could totter all the way to his food dish and litter box. I don't think his poor frostbitten feet had touched the ground all day.

The next morning, Doris Armstrong brought in a warm pink blanket. Doris was the grandparent on staff, our mother hen. We all watched as she bent down and scratched the kitten under the chin, then folded the blanket and put it in a cardboard box. The kitten stepped gingerly into the box and curled his legs underneath his body for warmth. His eyes closed in blissful contentment, but he had only a few seconds to rest before someone snatched him up and wrapped him in her arms. A few seconds, but it was enough. The staff had been polarized for years. Now we were all making accommodations, coming together as a family, and the kitten was clearly happy to call the library home.

It wasn't until late the second morning that we finally shared our little guy with someone outside the staff. That person was Mary Houston, Spencer's local historian and a member of the library board. The staff may already have accepted the kitten, but keeping him wasn't our decision. The previous day I had called the mayor, Squeege Chapman, who was in his last month in office. As I suspected, he didn't care. Squeege wasn't a reader; I'm not even sure he knew Spencer had a library. The city attorney, my second call, didn't know of any statutes barring animals from the library and didn't feel compelled to spend time looking for one. Good enough for me. The library board, a panel of citizens appointed by the mayor to oversee the library, had the final say. They didn't object to the idea of a library cat, but I can't say they were enthusiastic. Their response was more 'Let's give it a try' than 'Heck, yeah, we're behind you a hundred percent.'

That's why meeting a board member like Mary was so important. Agreeing to have an animal in the library was one thing; agreeing on *this* animal was another thing entirely. You can't just put any cute cat in a library. If he's not friendly, he's going to make enemies. If he's too shy or scared, nobody will stand up for him. If he's not patient, he's going to bite. If he's too rambunctious, he's going to make a mess. And above all, he has to love being around people, and he has to make those people love him back. In short, it has to be the right cat.

I had no doubt about our boy. From the moment he looked up into my eyes that first morning, so calm and content, I knew he was right for the library. There wasn't a flutter in his heart as I held him in my arms; there wasn't a moment of panic in his eyes. He trusted me completely. He trusted everyone on staff completely. That's what made him so special: his complete and unabashed trust. And because of it, I trusted him, too.

But that doesn't mean I wasn't a little apprehensive when I motioned Mary into the staff area. As I took the kitten in my arms and turned to face her, I felt a flutter in *my* heart, a moment of doubt. When the kitten had looked into my eyes, something else had happened, too; we had made a connection. He was more than just a cat to me. It had only been a day, but already I couldn't stand the thought of being without him.

'There he is,' Mary exclaimed with a smile. I held him a little more tightly as she reached out to pet him on the top of the head, but Dewey didn't even stiffen. Instead, he stretched out his neck to sniff her hand.

'Oh, my,' Mary said. 'He's handsome.'

Handsome. I heard it over and over again the next few days because there was no other way to describe him. This was a handsome cat. His coat was a mix of vibrant orange and white with subtle darker stripes. It grew longer as he got older, but as a kitten it was thick and stylishly long only around his neck. A lot of cats have pointy noses, or their mouths jut out a bit too far, or they're a little lopsided, but this kitten's face was perfectly proportioned. And his eyes, those huge golden eyes.

But it wasn't just his looks that made him beautiful; it was also his personality. If you cared at all about cats, you just had to hold him. There was something in his face, in the way he looked at you, that called out for love.

'He likes to be cradled,' I said, gently sliding him into Mary's arms. 'No, on his back. That's right. Like a baby.'

'A one-pound baby.'

'I don't think he even weighs that much.'

The kitten shook his tail and nestled down into Mary's arms. He didn't just trust the library staff instinctively, it turned out; he trusted everyone.

'Oh, Vicki,' Mary said. 'He's adorable. What's his name?'

'We're calling him Dewey. After Melville Dewey. But we haven't really decided on a name yet.'

'Hi, Dewey. Do you like the library?' Dewey stared into Mary's face, then pushed his head against her arm. Mary looked up with a smile. 'I could hold him all day.'

But, of course, she didn't. She put Dewey back into my arms, and I took him around the corner. The entire staff was waiting for us. 'That went well,' I said. 'One down, ten thousand to go.'

Slowly we started introducing Dewey to a few regulars known to love cats. He was still weak, so we passed him directly into their arms. Marcie Muckey came in that second day. Instantly smitten. Mike Baehr and his wife, Peg, loved him. 'This is a great idea,' they said, which was nice to hear since Mike was on the library board. Pat Jones and Judy Johnson thought him adorable. Actually there were four Judy Johnsons in Spencer. Two were regular library users, and both were Dewey fans. How big is a town of 10,000 people? Big enough to have four Judy Johnsons, three furniture stores, two commercial streets with stoplights, but only one mansion. Everyone calls it The Mansion. Typical Iowa – no fuss, no bother, just the facts.

A week later, Dewey's story ran on the front page of the *Spencer Daily Reporter* under the headline 'Purr-fect Addition Made to Spencer Library.' The article, which took up half the page, told the story of Dewey's miraculous rescue and was accompanied by a color photograph of a tiny orange kitten staring shyly but confidently into the camera from atop an old-fashioned pull-drawer card catalog.

Publicity is a dangerous thing. For a week, Dewey had been a secret between the library staff and a few select patrons. If you didn't come into the library, you didn't know about him. Now everyone in town knew. Most people, even library regulars, didn't give Dewey a second thought. There were two groups, though, that were thrilled by his arrival: the cat lovers and the children. Just the smiles on the faces of the children, their excitement and laughter, were enough to convince me Dewey should stay.

Then there were the complainers. I was a little disappointed, I must admit, but not surprised. There is nothing on God's green earth that someone won't complain about, including both God and green earth.

One woman took particular offense. Her letter, sent to me and every member of the city council, was pure fire and brimstone, full of images of children keeling over from sudden asthma attacks and pregnant mothers spontaneously miscarrying when exposed to kitty litter. According to the letter, I was a murderous madwoman who was not only threatening the health of every innocent child in town, born or unborn, but also destroying the social fabric of the community. An animal! In a library! If we let that stand, what was to stop people from walking a cow down Grand Avenue? In fact, she threatened to show up in the library one morning very soon with her cow in tow. Fortunately nobody took her seriously. I have no doubt she spoke for others in the community, in her overblown way, but general anger wasn't my concern. None of those people, as far as I could tell, ever visited the library.

Far more important to me, though, were the worried phone calls. 'My child has allergies. What am I going to do? He loves the library,' one woman said. I knew that would be the most common concern, so I was prepared. A year earlier, Muffin, the beloved cat-in-residence at the Putnam Valley Library in upstate New York, had been banished after a library board member developed a severe cat allergy. As a consequence, the library lost $80,000 in promised donations, mostly from the estates of local citizens. I had no intention of letting my cat, or my library, go the way of Muffin.

Spencer didn't have an allergist, so I solicited the advice of two general practice doctors. The Spencer Public Library, they noted, was a large, open space sectioned off by rows of four-foot-high shelves. The staff area, my office, and the supply closets were enclosed by a temporary wall, leaving six feet open to the ceiling. There were two door-size openings in that wall, and since neither had a door, they were always accessible. Even the staff area was an open space, with desks pushed back-to-back or separated by bookshelves.

Not only did this layout allow Dewey easy access to the safety of the staff area at all times, but the doctors assured me it would also prevent the buildup of dander and hair. The library, apparently, was perfectly designed to prevent allergies. If anyone on staff had been allergic it might have been a problem, but a few hours of exposure every couple of days? The doctors agreed there was nothing to worry about.

I spoke personally with each concerned caller and passed on this professional assessment. The parents were skeptical, of course, but most brought their children to the library for a trial run. I held Dewey in my arms for each visit. I not only didn't know how the parents would react, I didn't know how Dewey would react because the children were so excited to see him. Their mothers would tell them to be quiet, be gentle. The children would approach slowly, tentatively, and whisper, 'Hi, Dewey,' and then explode with squeals as their mothers ushered them away with a quick, 'That's enough.' Dewey didn't mind the noise; he was the calmest kitten I'd ever seen. He did mind, I think, that these children weren't allowed to pet him.

But a few days later, one family was back, this time with a camera. And this time the allergic little boy, the object of such concern for the mother, was sitting beside Dewey, petting him, while his mother took pictures.

'Justin can't have pets,' she told me. 'I never knew how much he missed them. He loves Dewey already.'

I loved Dewey already, too. We all loved Dewey. How could you resist his charm? He was beautiful, loving, social – and still limping on his tiny frostbitten feet. What I couldn't believe was how much Dewey loved us. How comfortable he seemed around strangers. His attitude seemed to be, how can anyone not love a cat? Or more simply, how can anyone resist me? Dewey didn't think of himself, I soon realized, as just another cat. He always thought of himself, correctly, as one of a kind.

3

Dewey Readmore Books

D ewey was a fortunate cat. He not only
survived the freezing library drop box, but
also fell into the arms of a staff that loved him
and a library perfectly designed to care for him. There
were no two ways about it, Dewey led a charmed life.
But Spencer was also lucky, because Dewey couldn't
have fallen into our lives at a better time. That winter
wasn't just bitterly cold; it was one of the worst times in
Spencer's history.

Those who lived in larger cities may not remember
the farm crisis of the 1980s. Maybe you remember Willie
Nelson and Farm Aid. Maybe you remember reading

about the collapse of family farming, about the nation moving from small growers to large factory farms that stretch for miles without a farmhouse, or even a farmworker, in sight. For most people, it was just a story, not something that affected them directly.

In Spencer, you could feel it: in the air, in the ground, in every spoken word. We had a solid manufacturing base, but we were still a farm town. We supported, and were supported by, farmers. And on the farms, things were falling apart. These were families we knew, families that had lived in the area for generations, and we could see the strain. First they stopped coming in for new parts and machinery, making do with bootstrap repairs. Then they cut back on supplies. Finally they stopped making mortgage payments, hoping for a booming harvest to set the account books right. When a miracle didn't come, the banks foreclosed. Almost half the farms in northwest Iowa went into foreclosure in the 1980s. Most of the new owners were giant farming conglomerates, out-of-state speculators, or insurance companies.

The farm crisis wasn't a natural disaster like the Dust Bowl of the 1930s. This was primarily a financial disaster. In 1978, farmland in Clay County was selling for $900 an acre. Then the price of land took off. In 1982, farmland was selling for $2,000 an acre. A year later, it was $4,000 an acre. Farmers borrowed up and bought more land. Why not, when the price was going up forever and you could make more money selling off land every few years than you could farming it?

Then the economy took a downturn. The price of land began to drop and credit dried up. The farmers couldn't borrow against their land to buy new machinery, or even new seed for the planting season. Crop prices weren't high enough to pay the interest on the old loans, many of which had rates of more than 20 percent a year. It took four or five years to reach bottom, years with false bottoms and false hopes, but economic forces were pulling our farmers steadily down.

In 1985, Land O'Lakes, the giant butter and margarine manufacturer, pulled out of the plant on the north edge of town. Soon after, unemployment reached 10 percent, which doesn't sound too bad until you realize that the population of Spencer had fallen from 11,000 to 8,000 in just a few years. The value of houses dropped 25 percent seemingly overnight. People were leaving the county, even the state of Iowa, looking for jobs.

The price of farmland plummeted further, forcing more farmers into foreclosure. But selling the land at auction couldn't cover the loans; the banks were stuck with the loss. These were rural banks, the backbones of small towns. They made loans to local farmers, men and women they knew and trusted. When the farmers couldn't pay, the system collapsed. In towns all across Iowa, banks failed. Banks were failing across the entire Midwest. The savings and loan in Spencer was sold to outsiders for pennies on the dollar, and the new owners didn't want to make new loans. Economic development stalled. As late as 1989, there wasn't a single housing permit issued in the city of Spencer. Not one. Nobody wanted to put money into a dying town.

Every Christmas, Spencer had a Santa Claus. The retailers sponsored a raffle and gave away a trip to Hawaii. In 1979, there wasn't a vacant storefront in town for Santa to set up shop in. In 1985, there were twenty-five empty storefronts downtown, a 30 percent vacancy rate. No trip to Hawaii was offered. Santa barely made it to town. There was a running joke: the last store owner out of downtown Spencer, please turn off the lights.

The library did what it could. When Land O'Lakes skipped town, we set up a job bank that contained all our job listings and books on job skills, job descriptions, and technical training. We set up a computer so local men and women could create résumés and cover letters. This was the first computer most of these people had ever seen. It was almost depressing how many people used the job bank. And if it was depressing for an employed librarian, just think how depressing it was for a laid-off factory worker, bankrupt small business owner, or out-of-work farmhand.

Then into our laps fell Dewey. I don't want to make too much of this one turn of events, because Dewey didn't put food on anyone's table. He didn't create jobs. He didn't turn our economy around. But one of the worst things about bad times is the effect on your mind. Bad times drain you of energy. They occupy your thoughts. They taint everything in your life. Bad news is as poisonous as bad bread. At the very least, Dewey was a distraction.

But he was so much more. Dewey's story resonated with the people of Spencer. We identified with it. Hadn't we all been shoved down the library drop box by the banks? By outside economic forces? By the rest of America, which ate our food but didn't care about the people who grew it?

Here was an alley cat, left for dead in a freezing drop box, terrified, alone, and clinging to life. He made it through that dark night, and that terrible event turned out to be the best thing that ever happened to him. He never lost his trust, no matter what the circumstances, or his appreciation for life. He was humble. Maybe *humble* isn't the right word – he was a cat, after all – but he wasn't arrogant. He was confident. Maybe it was the confidence of the near-death survivor, the serenity you find when you've been to the end, beyond hope, and made it back. All I knew was that, from the moment we found him, Dewey believed everything was going to be fine.

And when he was around, he made others believe that, too. It took him ten days to get healthy enough to explore the library on his own, and once he did it was clear he had no interest in books, shelves, and other inanimate objects. His interest was people. If there was a patron in the library, he'd walk straight up to him – still slow on his sore feet but no longer hobbling – and jump into his lap. More often than not he was pushed away, but rejection never deterred him. Dewey kept jumping, kept looking for laps to lie in and hands to pet him, and things started to change.

I noticed it first with the older patrons, who often came to the library to flip through magazines or browse for books. Once Dewey started spending time with them, they showed up more frequently and stayed longer. A few seemed better dressed, with more care given to their appearance. They had always given the staff a friendly wave or good morning, but now they engaged us in conversation, and that conversation was usually about Dewey. They couldn't get enough Dewey stories. They weren't just killing time now; they were visiting friends.

One older man in particular came in at the same time every morning, sat in the same big, comfortable chair, and read the newspaper. His wife had recently died, and I knew he was lonely. I didn't expect him to be a cat person, but from the first moment Dewey climbed into his lap the man was beaming. Suddenly he wasn't reading the newspaper alone. 'Are you happy here, Dewey?' the man would ask every morning as he petted his new friend. Dewey would shut his eyes and, more often than not, drop off to sleep.

And then there was the man at the job bank. I didn't know him personally, but I knew his type – proud, hardworking, resilient – and I knew he was suffering. He was from Spencer like most of the men who used the job bank, a laborer not a farmer. His job-hunting outfit, like his former work outfit, was jeans and a standard-issue shirt, and he never used the computer. He studied the résumé books; he looked through our job listings; he never asked for help. He was quiet, steady, unflappable, but as the weeks passed I could see the strain in the hunch of his back and the deepening lines on his always clean-shaven face. Every morning, Dewey approached him, but the man always pushed him away. Then one day I saw Dewey sitting on his lap, and for the first time in weeks the man was smiling. He was still bent, and there was still sadness in his eyes, but he was smiling. Maybe Dewey couldn't give much, but in the winter of 1988 he gave exactly what Spencer needed.

So I gave our kitten to the community. The staff understood. He wasn't our cat, not really. He belonged to the patrons of the Spencer Public Library. I put a box by the front door, right next to the job bank, and told people, 'You know the cat who sits on your lap and helps with your résumé? The one who reads the newspaper with you? Who steals the lipstick out of your purse and helps you find the fiction section? Well, he's your cat, and I want you to help name him.'

I had been library director for only six months, so I was still enthusiastic about contests. Every few weeks we put a box in the lobby, made an announcement on the local radio station, offered a prize for the winning entry, and tried to stoke interest in the latest bit of library news. A good contest with a good prize might draw fifty entries. If the prize was expensive, like a television set, we might scrape up seventy. Usually we got about twenty-five. Our Name the Kitty contest, which wasn't mentioned on the radio because I wanted only regular patrons to participate, and which didn't even offer a prize, received three hundred ninety-seven entries. Three hundred ninety-seven entries! That's when I realized the library had stumbled onto something important. Community interest in Dewey was off all our charts.

Lasagna-loving Garfield was at the height of his popularity, so Garfield was a popular choice. There were nine votes for Tiger. Tigger was almost as popular. Morris was another multiple vote-getter, after the Nine Lives spokescat. Even cultural blips like ALF (a cuddly alien puppet with his own television show) and Spuds (after Spuds MacKenzie, the hard-drinking party dog of beer commercial fame) received votes. There were a few mean-spirited entries, like Fleabag, and some that tripped over the thin line between clever and weird, like Catgang Amadeus Taffy (a sudden sweet tooth?), Ladybooks (an odd name for a male cat), Hopsnopper, Boxcar, and Nukster.

By far the most entries, more than fifty, were for Dewey. Apparently the patrons had already grown attached to this kitten, and they didn't want him to change. Not even his name. And to be honest, the staff didn't, either. We, too, had grown attached to Dewey just the way he was.

Still, the name needed something. Our best option, we decided, was to think of a last name. Mary Walk, our children's librarian, suggested Readmore. A commercial running during the Saturday morning cartoons – this was back when cartoons were only for children and shown only before noon on Saturdays – featured a cartoon cat named O.G. Readmore who encouraged kids to 'read a book and take a look at the TV in your head.' I'm sure that's where the name came from. Dewey Readmore. Close, but not quite. I suggested the last name Books.

Dewey Readmore Books. One name for the librarians, who live by the Dewey decimal system. One for the children. One for everyone.

Do We Read More Books? A challenge. A name to put us all in the mood to learn. The whole town was going to be well-read and well-informed in no time.

Dewey Readmore Books. Three names for our regal, confident, beautiful cat. I'm sure we'd have named him Sir Dewey Readmore Books if we had thought of it, but we were not only librarians, we were from Iowa. We didn't stand on pomp and circumstance. And neither did Dewey. He always went by his first name or, occasionally, just 'the Dew.'

4

A Day in the Library

C ats are creatures of habit, and it didn't take long for Dewey to develop a routine. When I arrived at the library every morning, he was waiting for me at the front door. He would take a few bites of his food while I hung up my jacket and bag, and then we would walk the library together, making sure everything was in place and discussing our evenings. Dewey was more a sniffer than a talker, but I didn't mind. The library, once so cold and dead first thing in the morning, was alive and well.

After our walk, Dewey would visit the staff. If someone was having a bad morning, he'd spend extra

time with her. Jean Hollis Clark had recently married
and commuted forty-five minutes from Estherville to
the library. You'd think that would frazzle her, but Jean
was the calmest person you've ever met. The only thing
that bothered her was the friction between a couple
of people on staff. She'd still be carrying the tension
when she arrived the next morning, and Dewey was
always there to comfort her. He had an amazing sense
of who needed him, and he was always willing to give
his time. But never for too long. At two minutes to
nine, Dewey would drop whatever he was doing and
race for the front door.

A patron was always waiting outside at nine o'clock
when we opened the doors, and she would usually
enter with a warm, 'Hi, Dewey. How are you this
morning?'

Welcome, welcome, I imagined him saying from his
post to the left of the door. *Why don't you pet the cat?*

No response. The early birds were usually there for
a reason, which meant they didn't have time to stop
and chat with a cat.

*No petting? Fine. There's always another person where
you came from – wherever that is.*

It wouldn't take long for him to find a lap, and
since he'd been up for two hours that usually meant
it was time for a quick nap. Dewey was already so
comfortable in the library he had no problem falling
asleep in public places. He preferred laps, of course,
but if they weren't available he would curl up in a
box. The cards for the catalog came in small boxes

about the size of a pair of baby shoes. Dewey liked to cram all four feet inside, sit down, and let his sides ooze over the edge. If the box was a little bigger, he buried his head and tail in the bottom. The only thing you could see was a big blob of back fur sticking out of the top. He looked like a muffin. One morning I found Dewey sleeping beside a box full of cards with one paw resting inside. It probably took him hours to reluctantly admit there wasn't room for anything else.

Soon after, I watched him slowly wind his way into a half-empty tissue box. He put his two front feet through the slit on top, then delicately stepped in with the other two. Slowly he sat down on his hind legs and rolled his back end until it was wedged into the box. Then he started bending his front legs and working the front of his body into the crease. The operation took four or five minutes, but finally there was nothing left but his head sticking out in one direction and his tail sticking out in the other. I watched as he stared half-lidded into the distance, pretending the rest of the world didn't exist.

In those days, Iowa provided envelopes with its tax forms, and we always put a box of them out for patrons. Dewey must have spent half his first winter curled up in that box. 'I need one envelope,' a patron would say nervously, 'but I don't want to disturb Dewey. What should I do?'

'Don't worry. He's asleep.'

'But won't it wake him up? He's lying on top of them.'

'Oh, no, Dew's dead to the world.'

The patron gently rolled Dewey to the side and then, far more carefully than necessary, slid out an envelope. He could have jerked it like a magician pulling a tablecloth from under a dinner setting, it wouldn't have mattered.

'Cat hair comes with the envelope, no charge.'

Dewey's other favorite resting spot was the back of the copier. 'Don't worry,' I told the confused patrons, 'you can't disturb him. He sleeps there because it's warm. The more copies you make, the more heat the machine produces, the happier he'll be.'

If the patrons weren't quite sure what to do with Dewey yet, the staff had no such hesitation. One of my first decisions was that no library funds, not one penny, would ever be spent on Dewey's care. Instead, we kept a Dewey Box in the back room. Everyone on staff tossed in their loose change. Most of us also brought in soda cans from home. Recycling soda cans was all the rage, and one of the clerks, Cynthia Behrends, would take the cans to a drop-off point every week. The whole staff was 'feeding the kitty' to feed the kitty.

In return for these small contributions, we'd get endless hours of pleasure. Dewey loved drawers, and he developed a habit of popping out of them when you least expected. If you were shelving books, he'd jump onto the cart and demand a trip around the library. And when Kim Peterson, the library secretary, started typing, you knew a show was about to begin.

As soon as I heard those keys, I'd put down my work and wait for the signal.

'Dewey's after the clacker thingies again!' Kim would call out.

I'd hurry out of my office to find Dewey hunched on the back edge of Kim's big white typewriter. His head would be jerking from side to side as the disk moved left to right, then back again, until finally he couldn't take it anymore and lunged at the clacker thingies, which were nothing more than the keys rising up to strike the paper. The whole staff would be there, watching and laughing. Dewey's antics always drew a crowd.

This was important. Everyone at the library was well-intentioned, but over the years the staff had become splintered and cliquish. Only Doris Armstrong, who was older and possibly wiser than the rest of us, had managed to stay friends with everyone. She had a large desk in the middle of the staff area where she covered each new book with a plastic protective sleeve, and her humor and good cheer held us together. She was also our biggest cat lover, and soon her desk was one of Dewey's favorite spots. He would sprawl there in the late morning, batting at her big sheets of plastic, the new center of attention and the mutual friend of everyone on staff. Here, finally, was something we could share. Just as important, he was a friend to all our children (or in Doris's case, grandchildren), too. Nothing concrete happened – no one apologized or discussed their issues, for instance – but once Dewey arrived the tension began to lift. We were laughing; we were happier; Dewey had brought us together.

But no matter how much fun Dewey was having, he never forgot his routine. At exactly ten thirty, he would hop up and head for the staff room. Jean Hollis Clark ate yogurt on her break, and if he hung around long enough she'd let him lick the lid. Jean was quiet and hardworking, but she always found ways to accommodate Dewey. If Dewey wanted downtime, he would lie limply over Jean's left shoulder – and only her left shoulder, never her right – while she filed papers. After a few months, Dewey wouldn't let us hold him cradled in our arms anymore (too much like a baby, I suppose) so the whole staff adopted Jean's over the shoulder technique. We called it the Dewey Carry.

Dewey helped me with downtime, too, which was nice since I had a tendency to work too hard. Many days I'd be hunched over my desk for hours, so intent on budget numbers or progress reports that I wouldn't even realize Dewey was there until he sprang into my lap.

'How you doing, baby boy?' I'd say with a smile. 'So nice to see you.' I'd pet him a few times before turning back to my work. Unsatisfied, he'd climb on my desk and start sniffing. 'Oh, you just happened to sit on the paper I'm working on, didn't you? Purely a coincidence.'

I put him on the floor. He hopped back up. 'Not now, Dewey. I'm busy.' I put him back down. He hopped back up. Maybe if I ignored him?

He pushed his head against my pencil. I pushed him aside. *Fine,* he thought, *I'll knock these pens to the ground.* Which he proceeded to do, one pen at a time, watching each one fall. I couldn't help but laugh.

'Okay, Dewey, you win.' I wadded up a piece of paper and threw it to him. He ran after it, sniffed it, then came back. Typical cat. Always one to play, never one to fetch. I walked over, picked up the paper, tossed it a few more times. 'What am I going to do with you?'

But it wasn't all jokes and games. I was the boss, and I had responsibilities – like giving the cat a bath. The first time I bathed Dewey, I was confident things would go well. He loved the bath that first morning, right? This time, Dewey slid into the sink like a block of ice dropped . . . into a vat of acid. He thrashed. He screamed. He put his feet on the edge of the sink and tried to throw his body over the side. I held him down with both arms. Twenty minutes later, I was covered with water. My hair looked like I had stuck my tongue in a light socket. Everybody laughed, including, eventually, me.

The third bath was just as bad. I managed to get Dewey scrubbed, but I didn't have the patience for toweling and blow-drying. Not this crazy kitten.

'Fine,' I told him. 'If you hate it that much, just go.'

Dewey was a vain cat. He would spend an hour washing his face until he got it just right. The funniest part was the way he would ball up his fist, lick it, and shove it into his ears. He would work those ears until they were sparkling white. Now, soaking wet, he looked like a Chihuahua crushed by a wave of toupees. It was pathetic. The staff was laughing and taking pictures, but Dewey looked so genuinely upset that after a few minutes the pictures stopped.

'Have a sense of humor, Dew,' I teased him. 'You brought this on yourself.' He curled up behind a shelf of books and didn't come out for hours. After that, Dewey and I agreed that two baths a year were plenty.

'The bath is nothing,' I told Dewey a few months into his stay at the library, wrapping him up in his green towel. 'You're not going to like this at all.' Dewey never rode in a cage; it was too much like that night in the box. Whenever I took him out of the library, I just wrapped him up in his green towel.

Five minutes later, we arrived at Dr. Esterly's office at the other end of town. There were several veterinarians in Spencer – after all, we lived in an area prone to breech-birth cows, distressed hogs, and sick farm dogs – but I preferred Dr. Esterly. He was a quiet, self-effacing man with an extremely deliberate way of speaking. His voice was deep and slow like a lazy river. He didn't rush. He was always tidy. He was a big man but his hands were gentle. He was conscientious and efficient. He knew his job. He loved animals. His authority came from his lack of words, not his use of them.

'Hi, Dewey,' he said, checking him over.

'Do you think this is absolutely necessary, Doctor?'

'Cats need to be neutered.'

I looked down at Dewey's tiny paws, which had finally healed. There were tuffs of fur sticking out from between his toes. 'Do you think he's part Persian?'

Dr. Esterley looked at Dewey. His regal bearing. The glorious ruff of long orange fur around his neck. He was a lion in alley cat clothing.

'No. He's just a good-looking alley cat.'

I didn't believe it for a second.

'Dewey is a product of survival of the fittest,' Dr. Esterly continued. 'His ancestors have probably lived in that alley for generations.'

'So he's one of us.'

Dr. Esterly smiled. 'I suppose so.' He picked Dewey up and held him under his arm. Dewey was relaxed and purring. The last thing Dr. Esterly said before they disappeared around the corner was, 'Dewey is one fine cat.'

He sure was. And I missed him already.

When I picked Dewey up the next morning, my heart almost broke in two. He had a faraway look in his eyes, and a little shaved belly. I took him in my arms. He pushed his head against my arm and started purring. He was so happy to see his old pal Vicki.

Back at the library, the staff dropped everything. 'Poor baby. Poor baby.' I gave him over to their care – he was our mutual friend, after all – and went back to work. One more set of hands and he might be crushed. Besides, the trip to the vet's office had put me behind, and I had a mountain of work. I needed two of me to do this job right, but the city would never have paid for it, so I was stuck with myself.

But I wasn't alone. An hour later, as I was hanging up the phone, I looked up to see Dewey hobbling through my office door. I knew he'd been getting love and attention from the rest of the staff, but I could tell from his determined wobbling that he needed something more.

Sure, cats can be fun, but my relationship with Dewey was already far more complex and intimate. He was so intelligent. He was so playful. He treated people so well. I didn't yet have a deep bond with him, but even now, near the beginning, I loved him.

And he loved me back. Not like he loved everyone else, but in a special and deeper way. The look he gave me that first morning meant something. It really did. Never was that more clear than now, as he pushed toward me with such determination. I could almost hear him saying, *Where have you been? I missed you*.

I reached down, scooped him up, and cradled him against my chest. I don't know if I said it out loud or to myself, but it didn't matter. Dewey could already read my moods, if not my mind. 'I'm your momma, aren't I?'

Dewey put his head on my shoulder, right up against my neck, and purred.

5

Catnip and Rubber Bands

Don't get me wrong, everything wasn't perfect with the Dew. Yes, he was a sweet and beautiful cat, and yes, he was extraordinarily trusting and generous, but he was still a kitten. He'd streak maniacally through the staff room. He'd knock your work to the floor out of pure playfulness. He was too immature to know who really needed him, and he sometimes wouldn't take no for an answer when a patron wanted to be left alone. At Story Hour, his presence made the children so rambunctious and unpredictable that Mary Walk, our children's librarian, banned him from the room. Then there was Mark, a large puppet of a child with muscular dystrophy. We used Mark to teach schoolchildren about disabilities. There was so much cat hair on Mark's legs that we finally had to put him in a closet. Dewey worked all night until he figured out how to open that closet and went right back to sleeping on Mark's lap. We bought a lock for the closet the next day.

But nothing compared to his behavior around catnip. Doris Armstrong was always bringing Dewey presents, such as little balls or toy mice. Doris had cats of her own, and like the consummate mother hen she always thought of Dewey when she went to the pet store for their litter and food. One day near the end of Dewey's first summer, she quite innocently brought in a bag of fresh catnip. Dewey was so excited by the smell I thought he was going to climb her leg. For the first time in his life, the cat actually begged.

When Doris finally crumbled a few leaves on the floor, Dewey went crazy. He started smelling them so hard I thought he was going to inhale the floor. After a few sniffs, he started sneezing, but he didn't slow down. Instead, he started chewing the leaves, then alternating back and forth: chewing, sniffing, chewing, sniffing. His muscles started to ripple, a slow cascade of tension flowing out of his bones and down his back. When he finally shook that tension out the end of his tail, he flopped over on the ground and rolled back and forth in the catnip. He rolled until he lost every bone in his body. Unable to walk, he slithered on the floor, undulating as he rubbed his chin along the carpet like a snowplow blade. I mean, the cat oozed. Then, gradually, his spine bent backward, in slow motion, until his head was resting on his behind. He formed figure eights, zigzags, pretzels. I swear the front half of his body wasn't even connected to the back half. When he finally, and accidentally, ended up flat on his tummy, he rippled his way back to the catnip and started rolling in it again. Most of the leaves were by now stuck in his fur, but he kept sniffing and chewing. Finally he stretched out on his back and started kicking his chin with his back legs. This lasted until, with a few flailing kicks hanging feebly in the air, Dewey passed out right on top of the last of the catnip. Doris and I looked at each other in amazement, then burst out laughing. My goodness, it was funny.

Dewey never tired of catnip. He would often sniff halfheartedly at old, worn-out leaves, but if there were fresh leaves in the library, Dewey knew it. And every time he got hold of catnip, it was the same thing: the undulating back, the rolling, the slithering, the bending, the kicking, and finally one very tired, very comatose cat. We called it the Dewey Mambo.

Dewey's other interest – besides puppets, drawers, boxes, copiers, typewriters, and catnip – was rubber bands. Dewey was absolutely fanatical about rubber bands. He didn't even need to see them; he could smell them across the library. As soon as you put a box of rubber bands on your desk, he was there.

'Here you go, Dewey,' I would say as I opened a new bag. 'One for you and one for me.' He would take his rubber band in his mouth and happily skip away.

I would find it the next morning . . . in his litter box. It looked like a worm poking its head out of a chunk of dirt. I thought, 'That can't be good.'

Dewey always attended staff meetings, but fortunately he wasn't yet able to understand what we were talking about. A few years down the road that cat and I were able to have long philosophical conversations, but for right now it was easy to wrap up the meeting with a simple reminder. 'Don't give Dewey any more rubber bands. I don't care how much he begs. He's been eating them, and I have a feeling rubber isn't the healthiest food for a growing kitten.'

The next day, there were more rubber band worms in Dewey's litter. And the next. And the next. At the next staff meeting, I was more direct. 'Is anyone giving Dewey rubber bands?'

No. No. No. No. No.

'Then he must be stealing them. From now on, don't leave rubber bands lying out on your desk.'

Easier said than done. Much, much easier said than done. You would be amazed how many rubber bands there are in a library. We all put our rubber band holders away, but that didn't even dent the problem. Rubber bands apparently are sneaky critters. They slide under computer keyboards and crawl into your pencil holder. They fall under your desk and hide in the wires. One evening I caught Dewey rummaging through a stack of work on someone's desk. There was a rubber band lurking every time he pushed a piece of paper aside.

'Even the hidden ones need to go,' I said at the next staff meeting. 'Let's clean up those desks and put them away. Remember, Dewey can smell rubber.' In a few days, the staff area looked neater than it had in years.

So Dewey started raiding the rubber bands left out on the circulation desk for patrons. We stashed them in a drawer. He found the rubber bands by the copier, too. The patrons were just going to have to ask for rubber bands. A small price to pay, I thought, in exchange for a cat who spent most of his day trying to make them happy.

Soon, our counteroperation was showing signs of success. There were still worms in the litter box but not nearly as many. And Dewey was being forced into brazenness. Every time I pulled out a rubber band, he was watching me.

'Getting desperate, are we?'

No, no, just seeing what's going on.

As soon as I put the rubber band down, Dewey pounced. I pushed him away, and he sat on the desk waiting for his chance. 'Not this time, Dewey,' I said with a grin. I admit it, this game was fun.

Dewey became more subtle. He waited for you to turn your back, then pounced on the rubber band left innocently lying on your desk. It had been there five minutes. Humans forget. Not cats. Dewey remembered every drawer left open a crack, then came back that night to wiggle his way inside. He never messed up the contents of the drawer. The next morning, the rubber bands were simply gone.

One afternoon I was walking past our big floor-to-ceiling supply cabinet. I was focused on something else, probably budget numbers, and only noticed the open door out of the corner of my eye. 'Did I just see . . .'

I turned around and walked back to the cabinet. Sure enough, there was Dewey, sitting on a shelf at eye level, a huge rubber band hanging out of his mouth.

You can't stop the Dew! I'm going to be feasting for a week.

I had to laugh. In general, Dewey was the best-behaved kitten I had ever seen. He never knocked books or displays off shelves. If I told him not to do something, he usually stopped. He was unfailingly kind to stranger and staffer alike. For a kitten, he was downright mellow. But he was absolutely incorrigible when it came to rubber bands. The cat would go anywhere and do anything to sink his teeth into a rubber band.

'Hold on, Dewey,' I told him, putting down my pile of work. 'I'm going to get a picture of this.' By the time I got back with the camera, the cat and his rubber band were gone.

'Make sure all the cabinets and drawers are completely closed,' I reminded the staff. Dewey was already notorious. He had a habit of getting closed inside cabinets and drawers and then leaping out at the next person to open them. We weren't sure if it was a game or an accident, but Dewey clearly enjoyed it.

A few mornings later I found file cards sitting suspiciously unbound on the front desk. Dewey had never gone for tight rubber bands before; now, he was biting them off every night. As always, he was delicate even in defiance. He left perfectly neat stacks, not a card out of place. The cards went into the drawers; the drawers were shut tight.

By the fall of 1988, you could spend an entire day in the Spencer Public Library without seeing a rubber band. Oh, they were still there, but they were squirreled away where only those with an opposable thumb could get to them. It was the ultimate cleaning operation. The library looked beautiful, and we were proud of our accomplishment. Except for one problem: Dewey was still chewing rubber bands.

I put together a crack investigative team to follow all leads. It took us two days to find Dewey's last good source: the coffee mug on Mary Walk's desk.

'Mary,' I said, flipping a notebook like the police detective in a bad television drama, 'we have reason to believe the rubber bands are coming from your mug.'

'That's impossible. I've never seen Dewey around my desk.'

'Evidence suggests the suspect is intentionally avoiding your desk to throw us off the trail. We believe he only approaches the mug at night.'

'What evidence?'

I pointed to several small pieces of chewed rubber band on the floor. 'He chews them up and spits them out. He eats them for breakfast. I think you know all the usual clichés.'

Mary shuddered at the thought of the garbage on the floor having passed into and out of the stomach of a cat. Still, it seemed so improbable. . . .

'The mug is six inches deep. It's full of paper clips, staples, pens, pencils. How could he possibly pluck out rubber bands without knocking everything over?'

'Where there's a will, there's a way. And this suspect has proven, in his eight months at the library, that he has the will.'

'But there are hardly any rubber bands in there! Surely this isn't his only source!'

'How about an experiment? You put the mug in the cabinet, we'll see if he pukes rubber bands near your desk.'

'But this mug has my children's pictures on it!'

'Good point. How about we just remove the rubber bands?'

Mary decided to put a lid on the mug. The next morning, the lid was lying on her desk with suspicious teeth marks along one edge. No doubt about it, the mug was the source. The rubber bands went into a drawer. Convenience was sacrificed for the greater good.

We never completely succeeded in wiping out Dewey's rubber band fixation. He'd lose interest, only to go back on the prowl a few months or even a few years later. In the end, it was more a game than a battle, a contest of wits and guile. While we had the wits, Dewey had the guile. And the will. He was far more intent on eating rubber bands than we were on stopping him. And he had that powerful, rubber-sniffing nose.

But let's not make too much of it all. Rubber bands were a hobby. Catnip and boxes were mere distractions. Dewey's true love was people, and there was nothing he wouldn't do for his adoring public. I remember standing at the circulation desk one morning talking with Doris when we noticed a toddler wobbling by. She must have recently learned to walk, because her balance was shaky and her steps uneven. It wasn't helping that her arms were wrapped tightly across her chest, clutching Dewey in a bear hug. His rear and tail were sticking up in her face, and his head was hanging down toward the floor. Doris and I stopped talking and watched in amazement as the little girl toddled in slow motion across the library, a very big smile on her face and a very resigned cat hanging upside down from her arms.

'Amazing,' Doris said.

'I should do something about that,' I said. But I didn't. I knew that, despite appearances, Dewey was completely in control of the situation. He knew what he was doing and, no matter what happened, he could take care of himself.

We think of a library, or any single building really, as a small place. How can you spend all day, every day, in a 13,000-square-foot room and not get bored? But to Dewey, the Spencer Public Library was a huge world full of drawers, cabinets, bookshelves, display cases, rubber bands, typewriters, copiers, tables, chairs, backpacks, purses, and a steady stream of hands to pet him, legs to rub against, and mouths to sing his praises. And laps. The library was always graciously, gorgeously full of laps.

By the fall of 1988, Dewey considered all of it his.

6

Moneta

S ize is a matter of perspective. For an insect, one stalk of corn, or even one ear of corn, can be the whole world. For Dewey, the Spencer Public Library was a labyrinth that kept him endlessly fascinated – at least until he started to wonder what was outside the front door. For most of the people in northwest Iowa, Spencer is the big city. In fact, we are the biggest city for a hundred miles in any direction. People from nine counties funnel into Spencer for entertainment and shopping. We have stores, services, live music, local theater, and, of course, the county fair. What more do you need? If there was a front door leading from Grand Avenue to the rest of the world, most people around here wouldn't have any interest in going through it.

In junior high school, I remember being scared of girls from Spencer, not because I'd ever met any but because they were from the big city. Like most people around here, I grew up on a farm. My great-great-aunt Luna was the first schoolteacher in Clay County. She taught class out of a one-room sod house. There have never been trees out here on the prairie, so the settlers built with what they could find: grass. Roots, soil, and all. My great-grandfather Norman Jipson was the one who amassed enough land to grant a farmstead to each of his six children. No matter where I went as a kid, I was surrounded by my father's family. Most of the Jipsons were staunch Baptists, and they didn't wear pants. All right, the men wore pants. Religiously. The women wore dresses. I never saw a pair of slacks on any woman on my father's side.

In time, my father inherited his land and started the hard work of running a family farm, but first he learned to dance. Dancing was off-limits to most Baptists, but Verlyn 'Jipp' Jipson was fifteen years younger than his four siblings, and his parents indulged him. As a young man, Jipp would slip out and drive the truck an hour to the Roof Garden, a 1920s gilded-era resort on the edge of Lake Okoboji, for their Friday-night dances. Okoboji is a mystical name in Iowa. West Okoboji, the centerpiece of a chain of five lakes, is the only blue-water, spring-fed lake in the state, and people come from Nebraska and even Minnesota, a state with a few lakes of its own, to the hotels along its shore. In the late 1940s, the hottest spot in the area, maybe even the whole state of Iowa, was the Roof Garden. Every big-name swing band played the joint, and often the ballroom was so packed you couldn't move. World War II was over, and the party seemed like it would go on forever. Outside, on the boardwalk, there was a roller coaster, a Ferris wheel, and enough lights, sounds, and pretty girls to make you forget that Lake Okoboji was a brilliant blue pinprick in the vast emptiness of the Great American Plains.

And there, in that little circle of light, Jipp Jipson met Marie Mayou. They danced the night away, and just about every other night for the next six months. My father kept the relationship a secret because he knew his family would never approve. The Mayous weren't like the Jipsons. They were full-blooded French by way of Montreal, and they were fiery, passionate people. They loved hard, fought hard, drank hard, and even churched hard, with a no-nonsense midwestern Catholicism that almost scorched the earth.

The Mayous owned the town café in Royal, Iowa, about ten miles from Dad's farm. My mother's father was a wonderful man: gregarious, honest, kind. He was also a full-blown alcoholic. As a child, Mom would leave school to work the lunch rush, then head back to school for a few hours in the afternoon. Often her father would be passed out in one of the booths, so Mom would have to get him off to bed and out of the way of the paying customers.

It wasn't that Marie Mayou's family was notorious. Ten miles was a long way in 1940s Iowa. The problem was that they were Catholic. So Mom and Dad ran away to Minnesota to get married. The wound from the elopement took a few years to heal, but practical always prevails in Iowa. If a deed is done, it's time to move on. Mom and Dad settled down on the family farm and soon had the first three of their six children, two boys (David and Mike) and a girl. I was the middle child.

The family farm. The idea has been romanticized, but for most of the history of the world family farming has been a difficult, poorly paid, backbreaking enterprise. The Jipson farm was no different. We had a cold water hand pump in the kitchen that you physically had to prime. We had a washing machine in the root cellar, but you had to heat the water on the stove upstairs. After the clothes were washed, you cranked them one by one through rollers to wring out the excess water, then hung them outside on the line. We had a shower in the corner of the root cellar. The walls were concrete, but we had tile on the floor. That was our luxury.

Air-conditioning? I didn't know such a thing existed. Mom worked in her kitchen six hours a day over an open flame, even in hundred-degree heat. The kids slept upstairs, and it was so hot on humid summer nights we'd take our pillows downstairs and sleep on the dining room floor. Linoleum was the coolest surface in the house.

Indoor plumbing? Until I was ten years old, we used a one-hole outhouse. When the outhouse became full, you simply dug a new hole and moved the shack. Hard to believe now, looking back, but it's true.

It was the best childhood, the very best. I wouldn't trade it for all the money in Des Moines. Why worry about new toys and clothes? No one we knew had those. We handed down clothes. We handed down toys. There was no television, so we talked to each other. Our big trip was once a year to the municipal swimming pool in Spencer. Every morning we woke up together, and then we worked together.

When I was ten, Mom and Dad had their second set of three children – Steven, Val, and Doug. I raised those children alongside Mom. We were Jipsons. We were there for each other. It's dark on a farm at night, and empty, and lonely, but I knew there was nothing out there in the world that could harm me – not Russians, not rockets, not thieves. I had my family. And if things got really bad, I had the cornfield. I could always run into it and disappear.

We weren't really alone, of course. Each square mile of farmland, bordered on all sides by those perfectly straight Iowa roads, was called a section. In those days, most sections held four family-owned farms. Three and a half of the families in our section were Catholic (we were the half), and there were seventeen children among them, so we had our own

baseball game. Even if only four kids showed up, we
played baseball. I can't remember thinking about
any other game. I was small, but by the time I was
twelve, I could hit a baseball across the ditch and into
the corn. Every night we huddled around the Jipson
family table and gave thanks to God that we'd gone
another day without losing our baseball in the corn.

Two miles from our eastern field, at the end of
the second section, was the town of Moneta, Iowa.
Spencer and Moneta were only twenty miles apart, but
they might as well have been different worlds. Some
might call that twenty-mile stretch nondescript, but if
you drive it in September, when the sky is darkening
with blue storm clouds and the crops form patches in
every glorious shade of brown, you'd be hard-pressed
not to call it beautiful. The highlight is probably the
faded wooden billboard outside the town of Everly
saluting the 1966 Iowa Girl's Basketball Champions.
I remember that team. Everly beat us by a point in the
regional finals, which were held in Spencer. I'd tell
you about the game, but it's already taken longer to
mention the sign than it takes to pass through Everly,
which has only five hundred people.

The population of Moneta never reached five
hundred, but it topped that number if you included
all the farmers, like my family, who thought of
themselves as members of that wonderful community.
In the 1930s, Moneta was the gambling capital of
northwest Iowa. The restaurant on Main Street was a
speakeasy, and there was a gambling hall in the back

accessible through a secret door. By the time I was a child, those legends were long gone, replaced in our imaginations by the baseball field and the bees. Every community has something the children remember. Come to Spencer in sixty years and the older people will say, 'We had a cat. He lived in the library. What was his name? Oh, yes, Dewey. I'll always remember Dewey.' In Moneta, it was the bees. A local family had sixty hives, and the honey was famous in four counties, which seemed like the whole world.

The centerpiece of town, though, was the Moneta School, a ten-room, two-story redbrick building just down the road from the baseball field. Almost everyone in town had attended the Moneta School, at least for a few years. There were only eight children in my grade, but what we lacked in size we made up for in amenities. Two local women cooked homemade meals for the whole school every day. Janet and I, the only girls in our class, often got special permission to go over in the morning and frost the cinnamon rolls. If you had a problem, a teacher would walk you to the hidden circle in the grove of trees behind the school where you could talk it out one-on-one. If you wanted to be alone, or with a special someone, you went to the grove, too. That's where I got my first kiss. The Moneta School had a party at the end of every school year with sack races, horse races, and, of course, baseball games. The whole town brought picnics. Everybody participated. In the middle of the summer, when the corn was so high it surrounded the town like a wall, there was the Moneta School reunion, which in the 1950s drew several thousand people. Everyone was proud of that school. Everyone.

Then, in 1959, the state of Iowa shuttered the Moneta School. The town had been on a long population slide, and the state could no longer justify the expense. Moneta had always been a hub for local farmers, but farming was changing. In the early 1950s, the first generation of giant harvesters and combines allowed farmers to plow and harvest larger fields. Some farmers bought new machines, then bought out their neighbors and doubled their production, then used that money to buy out more neighbors. Farm families began to disappear, moving away to local population centers like Spencer, and with them went the farmhouses, the family gardens, and the rows of trees the original settlers had planted to protect the house from the summer sun and the winter wind. These were huge trees, five feet around and a hundred years old. When larger farmers moved in, they bulldozed everything – trees, buildings, everything – piled it up, and burned it to the ground. Why keep a house nobody's living in when you could have a field? The land went back, but not to nature. It went to corn.

The old family farmers raised livestock. They planted gardens. They grew crops in distinct, smaller fields. On the large new farms, there was only corn and its companion crop, soybeans. Every year Iowa grew more corn, but we ate less and less of the crop, at least as kernels and cobs. Most was used as animal feed. Some eventually became ethanol. The rest was separated, broken down, and processed. Have you ever wondered what xanthan gum is? It's processed corn, like almost everything else in that long list of unidentifiable ingredients printed on the packaging of your dinner. Seventy percent of the average American diet – 70 percent! – is corn.

But life in farm country isn't easy. A few large farms are worth a fortune, but for most farmers and the people who rely on them – farmhands, salesmen, storage facilities, processing plants, local merchants – the money is tight, the work is hard, and life is often beyond your control. If it doesn't rain; if it doesn't stop raining; if it gets too hot or too cold; if prices don't hold up when your product hits market, there's not much you can do. Farm life isn't forty acres and a mule anymore. Farmers need large combines to plow big fields, and they can cost $500,000 or more. Throw in seed, chemicals, and living expenses, and a farmer's debt can easily top a million. If they stumble, or fall behind the times, or simply have a run of bad luck, most can't make it.

The same is true of the towns in farm country. Towns are, after all, a collection of people. The town relies on the people; the people rely on the town. Like the pollen and the corn silk, they are interdependent. That's why the people of northwest Iowa take such pride in their towns. That's why they invest so much energy in making their towns work. They plant trees;

they build parks; they join community organizations. They know if a town is not constantly looking ahead, it can fall behind, and then it can die.

Some people think the grain elevator burning down in the 1930s ruined the town of Moneta. I think it was the closing of the Moneta School. After the Jipson kids started being bused ten miles away to Hartley in 1959, Dad lost interest in struggling against the farm. Our land didn't produce, and Dad couldn't afford big new machinery. He joined a cattle-buying business, then started selling insurance. The Jipsons had been on the farmstead for three generations, but two years after the Moneta School closed Dad sold out to a neighbor and went into insurance full-time. He hated it, hated having to use scare tactics and lowball families in their time of need. He ended up working as a salesman for Crow brand seed. The neighbor who bought our land leveled our farmhouse, chopped down our trees, and turned the entire 160 acres into farmland. He even straightened the creek. I often drive by now without even recognizing it. The first four feet of our dirt driveway is all that remains of my childhood.

Drive fifteen miles west of Spencer today and there's still a sign on the side of the road for Moneta. Turn left. Two miles down the pavement ends, leaving only a dirt track running between the fields. But there isn't a town. There are maybe fifteen houses, at least half of them abandoned. There isn't a single business to be seen. Almost all the buildings on the old downtown strip I remember from my childhood are gone, replaced by a cornfield. You can stand at the former spot of the Moneta general store, where kids would stand transfixed in front of the giant counter full of penny candies and whistles, and watch the cultivators, cone-shaped chutes in front and barrels of fertilizer and poison strapped on the back, crawl across fields like tiny grasshoppers tiptoeing across a vast emptiness. The dance hall remains, and the old speakeasy, but both are shuttered. In a few years, they'll probably be gone, too.

The Moneta School still stands behind, but volunteer trees are growing between the bricks. Most of the windows are broken. Goats lived in the building for a decade, wrecking the floors and biting holes in the walls, and you can still smell them. The only thing left is the reunion. Forty years after the closing of the Moneta School, the annual reunion still drew a thousand people a year back to the field where we used to hold those baseball games and end-of-the-year parties. Now the reunion is down to a hundred or so. The school has been closed fifty years; there aren't that many graduates left. Soon the sign on Highway 18 will be the last thing standing, still pointing two miles down the lonely road to Moneta.

7

Grand Avenue

The farm crisis of the 1980s was hard, but most of us never truly believed Spencer would go the way of Moneta. We never believed it would give up, blow away, disappear. Throughout its history, after all, the town had proved its resilience. Nothing had ever been handed to Spencer or its citizens. What we'd gotten, we'd earned.

Spencer started as a sham town. In the 1850s, a developer sold numbered lots on a large parcel near a bend in the Little Sioux River. The settlers expected a prosperous town in a fertile river valley, but they never found it. There was nothing but a lazy river and a single cabin – four miles away. The only place a town existed was on paper.

The homesteaders decided to stay. Instead of coming to an established town, they scratched a community out of the dirt. Spencer incorporated in 1871 and immediately petitioned the government for a railroad depot, which it wouldn't get for almost fifty years. Later that year, it wrested the seat of Clay County away from Petersen, a larger town thirty miles to the south. Spencer was a blue-collar town. It didn't have pretensions, but it knew that out here on the Plains you have to keep moving, modernizing, and growing.

In June 1873, the grasshoppers arrived, devouring the crops down to the stalks before moving on to the harvested grain. In May 1874, the grasshoppers returned. They came again in July 1876, just as the wheat was ripening and the corn coming into tassel and silk. As described in *The Spencer Centennial*, an account of the community written for our hundredth anniversary, 'the grasshoppers ate the heads off the grain and settled on the corn until they broke it down with their weight. There was complete destruction.'

Farmers abandoned the area. Town residents turned their homes and businesses over to their creditors and left the county. Those who remained pulled together and helped one another through a long and hungry winter. In the spring they scraped together enough credit to buy seed for a full planting. The grasshoppers ate their way to the western edge of Clay County, about forty miles away, but they came no farther. The crop of 1877 was the best the area had ever produced. The grasshoppers never returned.

When the first generation of homesteaders became too old to farm, they moved into Spencer. They built small Craftsman bungalows north of the river, mixing with the merchants and hired hands. When the railroad finally arrived, local farmers no longer had to drive a horse and buggy fifty miles to market. Now other farmers drove twenty miles to Spencer. The town celebrated by widening the road from the river to the train depot. Those eight blocks, christened Grand Avenue, became the main retail corridor for the entire region. There was a savings and loan downtown, a popcorn factory on the north side near the fairgrounds, a concrete block factory, a brick works, and a lumberyard. But Spencer was not an industrial town. There were no large industrial facilities. There were no diamond-studded, twenty-dollar-bill-smoking frontier financiers. There was no row of Victorian mansions. There were the fields, the farmers, and the eight blocks of businesses under our enormous blue Iowa sky.

And then came June 27, 1931.

The temperature was 103 degrees when, at 1:36 p.m., an eight-year-old boy lit a sparkler outside Otto Bjornstad's drugstore at Main and West Fourth Street. Someone screamed, and the startled boy dropped the sparkler into a large display of fireworks.

The display exploded and the fire, whipped by a hot wind, spread across the street. Within minutes the blaze was burning down both sides of Grand Avenue, completely beyond the control of Spencer's small fire department. Fourteen surrounding towns sent equipment and men, but water pressure was so low river water had to be pumped into the mains. At the height of the blaze, the pavement on Grand Avenue caught fire. By the end of the day, thirty-six buildings housing seventy-two businesses, well more than half the businesses in town, were destroyed.

I can't imagine what those people were thinking as they looked at the smoke floating out over the fields and the smoldering remains of their beloved town. That afternoon northwest Iowa must have felt like a lonely, isolated place. Out here, towns die. The businesses shutter; the people move on. Most of the families in Spencer had scratched out a living in the area for three generations. Now, on the cusp of the Great Depression – it had already started on the coasts but wouldn't spread to inland areas like northwest Iowa until the mid-1930s – Spencer's heart was in ashes. The cost, just over $2,000,000 in Depression-era dollars, makes it still the most expensive man-made disaster in the history of Iowa.

How do I know all this? Everyone in Spencer knows it. The fire is our legacy. It defines us. The only thing we don't know is the name of the boy who started the fire. Somebody knows it, of course, but a decision was made to keep the identity secret. The message:

we're a town. We're in this together. Let's not point a finger. Let's fix the problem. Around here, we call that progressive. If you ask anyone in Spencer about the town, they'll tell you, 'It's progressive.' That's our mantra. If you ask what *progressive* means, we'll say, 'We have parks. We volunteer. We always look to improve.' If you dig deeper, we'll think for a minute and finally say, 'Well, there was a fire. . . .'

It's not the fire that defines us; it's what the town did afterward. Two days after the fire, a commission was meeting to make the new downtown as modern and accident–proof as possible, even as stores reopened out of houses and outbuildings. Nobody quit. Nobody said, 'Let's just put it back the way it was.' Our community leaders had traveled to the large cities of the Midwest, like Chicago and Minneapolis. They had seen the cohesive planning and sleek style of places like Kansas City. Within a month, a master plan was created for a modern Art Deco downtown in the style of the most prosperous cities of the day. Each destroyed building was individually owned, but each was also part of a town. The owners bought into the plan. They understood that they lived, worked, and survived together.

If you visit downtown Spencer today, you might not think Art Deco. Most of the architects were from Des Moines and Sioux City, and they built in a style called Prairie Deco. The buildings are low to the ground. They are mostly brick. A few have Mission-style turrets, like the Alamo. Prairie Deco is a practical style. It's quiet but elegant. It's not flashy. It doesn't show off. It suits us. We like to be modern in Spencer, but we don't like to draw attention to ourselves.

When you come downtown, maybe for a pastry at Carroll's Bakery or shopping at The Hen House, you probably won't notice the low storefronts and long, clean lines. Instead, you'll park along Grand Avenue, stroll under the large flat overhangs and in front of the glass windows. You'll notice the metal streetlights and brick inlay on the sidewalks, the way the stores seem to flow one after the other, and you'll think to yourself, 'I like it here. This is a downtown that works.'

Our downtown is the legacy of the fire of 1931, but it is also the legacy of the farm crisis of the 1980s. When times are tough, you either pull together or fall apart. That's true of families, towns, even people. In the late 1980s, Spencer once again pulled together. And once again, the transformation occurred from the inside out when the merchants on Grand Avenue, many in stores run by their grandparents in 1931, decided they could make the city better. They hired a business manager for the entire downtown retail corridor; they made infrastructure improvements; they spent heavily on advertising even when there seemed to be no money left in the community to spend.

Slowly the wheels of progress began to turn. A local couple bought and began to restore The Hotel, the largest and most historic building in town. The run-down building had been an eyesore, a drain on our collective energy and goodwill. Now it became a source of pride, a promise of better days to come. Along the commercial section of Grand Avenue, the shopkeepers paid for new windows, better sidewalks, and summer-evening entertainment. They clearly believed the best days of Spencer were ahead, and when people came downtown, heard the music, and walked the new sidewalks, they believed it, too. And if that wasn't enough, at the south end of downtown, just around the corner on Third Street, was a clean, welcoming, newly remodeled library.

At least, that was my plan. As soon as I was made director in 1987, I started pressing for money to remodel the library. There was no city manager, and even mayor was a part-time, largely ceremonial position. The city council made all the decisions. So that's where I went, again and again and again.

The Spencer city council was a classic 'good ole boy' network, an extension of the power brokers who met at Sister's Café. Sister's was only twenty feet from the library, but I don't think a single member of that crowd had ever stepped foot in our building. Of course, I never frequented Sister's Café, so the problem cut both ways.

'Money for the library? What's that going to do? We need jobs, not books.'

'The library isn't a warehouse,' I told the council. 'It's a vital community center. We have job placement resources, meeting rooms, computers.'

'Computers! How much are we spending on computers?'

That was always the danger. Start asking for money and sooner or later someone was going to say, 'What does the library need money for, anyway? You've already got enough books.'

I told them, 'Newly paved roads are nice, but they don't lift our community's spirits. Not like a warm, friendly, welcoming library. Wouldn't it be great for morale to have a library we're proud of?'

'I got to be honest. I don't see how prettier books make a difference.'

After almost a year of being put on the shelf, I was frustrated, but certainly not defeated. Then a funny thing happened: Dewey started to make my argument for me. By the late summer of 1988, there was a noticeable change at the Spencer Public Library. Our visitor numbers were up. People were staying longer. They were leaving happy, and that happiness was being carried to their homes, their schools, and their places of employment. Even better, people were talking.

'I was down at the library,' someone would comment while window-shopping on the new, improved Grand Avenue.

'Was Dewey there?'

'Of course.'

'Did he sit in your lap? He always sits on my daughter's lap.'

'Actually, I was reaching for a book on a high shelf, not really paying attention, and instead of a book

I grabbed a handful of Dewey. I was so startled I dropped a book right on my toe.'

'What did Dewey do?'

'He laughed.'

'Really?'

'No, but I sure did.'

The conversation must have reached Sister's Café, because eventually even the city council started to notice. Slowly their attitude shifted. First they stopped laughing at me. Then they started listening.

'Vicki,' the city council finally said, 'maybe the library does make a difference. There's a financial crunch right now, as you know, and we don't have any money. But if you have the funds, you have our support.' It wasn't much, I admit, but it was the most the library had gotten from the city in a long, long time.

8

A Cat's Best Friends

The whisper the city council heard in the autumn of 1988 wasn't mine. Or at least not mine alone. It was the voice of the people bubbling up, the voices that were usually never heard: those of the older residents, the mothers, the children. Some patrons came to the library for a purpose – to check out a book, to read the newspaper, to find a magazine. Other patrons considered the library a destination. They enjoyed spending time there; they were sustained and strengthened. Every month there were more of these people. Dewey wasn't just a novelty; he was a fixture in the community. People came to the library to see him.

Not that Dewey was an especially fawning animal. He didn't just rush up to each person who came through the door. He made himself available at the front door if people wanted him; if they didn't, they could step around and be on their way. That's the subtle difference between dogs and cats, and especially a cat like Dewey: cats may need you, but they aren't needy.

When regular patrons came in and Dewey wasn't there to greet them, they often walked the library looking for him. First they searched the floor, figuring Dewey was hiding around a corner. Then they checked the top of the bookshelves.

'Oh, how are you, Dewey? I didn't see you there,' they would say, reaching up to pet him. Dewey would give them the top of his head to pet, but he wouldn't follow them. The patrons always looked disappointed.

But as soon as they forgot about him, Dewey jumped into their laps. That's when I saw the smiles. It wasn't just that Dewey sat with them for ten or fifteen minutes; it was that he had singled them out for special attention. By the end of his first year, dozens of patrons were telling me, 'I know Dewey likes everyone, but I have a special relationship with him.'

I smiled and nodded. 'That's right, Judy,' I thought. 'You and everyone else who comes into this library.'

Of course, if Judy Johnson (or Marcie Muckey or Pat Jones or any of Dewey's other fans) hung around long enough, she was sure to be disappointed. Many times I had that conversation only to see the smile drop half an hour later when, leaving the library, she happened to notice Dewey sitting on someone else's lap.

'Oh, Dewey,' Judy would say. 'I thought it was all about me.'

She would look at him for a few seconds, but Dewey wouldn't look up. Then she would smile. I knew what Judy was thinking. 'That's just his job. He still loves me best.'

Then there were the children. If you wanted to understand the effect Dewey had on Spencer, all you had to do was look at the children. The smiles when they came into the library, the joy as they searched and called for him, the excitement when they found him. Behind them, their mothers were smiling, too.

I knew families were suffering, that for many of these children times were hard. The parents never discussed their problems with me or anyone on staff. They probably didn't discuss them with their closest friends. That's not the way we are around here; we don't talk about our personal circumstances, be they good, bad, or indifferent. But you could tell. One boy wore his old coat from the previous winter. His mother stopped wearing her makeup and, eventually, her jewelry. The boy loved Dewey; he clung to Dewey like a true friend; and his mother never stopped smiling when she saw them together. Then, around October, the boy and his mother stopped coming to the library. The family, I found out, had moved away.

That wasn't the only boy who wore an old coat that fall, and he certainly wasn't the only child who loved Dewey. They all wanted, even craved, his attention, so much so that they learned enough control to spend Story Hour with him. Every Tuesday morning, the murmur of excited children in the Round Room, where Story Hour was held, would be suddenly punctuated by a cry of 'Dewey's here!' A mad rush would ensue as every child in the room tried to pet Dewey at the same time.

'If you don't settle down,' our children's librarian, Mary Walk, would tell them, 'Dewey has to go.'

A barely contained hush would fall over the room as the children took their seats, trying their best to contain their excitement. When they were relatively calm, Dewey would begin sliding between them, rubbing against each child and making them all giggle. Soon kids were grabbing at him and whispering, 'Sit with me, Dewey. Sit with me.'

'Children, don't make me warn you again.'

'Yes, Mary.' The children always called Mary Walk by her first name. She never got into the habit of Miss Mary.

Dewey, knowing he had pushed the limit, would stop wandering and curl up in the lap of one lucky child. He didn't let a child grab him and hold him in her lap; he *chose* to spend time with her. And every week it was a different child.

Once he had chosen a lap, Dewey usually sat quietly for the whole hour. Unless a movie was being shown. Then he would jump on a table, curl his legs under his body, and watch the screen intently. When the credits rolled he feigned boredom and jumped down. Before the children could ask, 'Where's Dewey?' he was gone.

There was only one child Dewey couldn't win over. She was four years old when Dewey arrived, and she came to the library every week with her mother and older brother. Her brother loved Dewey. The girl hung back as far as possible, looking tense and nervous. Her mother eventually confided in me that the girl was afraid of four-legged animals, especially cats and dogs.

What an opportunity! I knew Dewey could do for this girl what he had done for the children with cat allergies, who finally had a cat to spend time with. I suggested exposing her gently to Dewey, first by looking through the window at him and then with supervised meetings.

'This is an ideal job for our gentle, loving Dewey,' I told her mother. I was so enthusiastic, I even researched the best books to help the girl overcome her fear.

Her mother didn't want to go that route, so instead of trying to change the girl's feelings about cats, I accommodated her. When the girl came to the door and waved at the clerk on the front desk, we found Dewey and locked him in my office. Dewey hated being locked in my office, especially when patrons were in the library. *You don't have to do this*, I could hear him howling. *I know who she is! I won't go near her!*

I hated to lock him away, and I hated to miss the opportunity for Dewey to make this little girl's life better, but what could I do? 'Don't force it, Vicki,' I told myself. 'It will come.'

With that in mind I planned a low-key celebration for Dewey's first birthday: just a cake made out of cat food for Dewey, and a normal one for the patrons. We didn't know exactly when he was born, but Dr. Esterly had estimated he was eight weeks old when we found him, so we counted back to late November and chose the eighteenth. We found Dewey on January 18, so we figured that was his lucky day.

A week before the celebration, we put out a card for signatures. Within days there were more than a hundred. At the next Story Hour, the children colored pictures of birthday cakes. Four days before the party, we strung the pictures on a clothesline behind the circulation desk. Then the newspaper ran a story, and we started receiving birthday cards in the mail. I couldn't believe it, people were sending birthday cards to a cat!

By the time the party rolled around, the kids were jumping up and down with excitement. Another cat would have been frightened, no doubt, but Dewey took it all in with his usual calm. Instead of interacting with the kids, though, he kept his eyes on the prize: his cat-food cake in the shape of a mouse, covered with Jean Hollis Clark's brand of full-fat yogurt (Dewey hated the diet-stuff). As the kids smiled and giggled, I looked out at the adults gathered at the back of the crowd, most of them parents. They were smiling as much as the children. Once again I realized how special Dewey was. Not just any cat would have this kind of fan club. And I realized a few other things, too: that Dewey was having an impact; that he had been accepted as part of the community; and that although I spent all day with him I would never know all the relationships he developed and all the people he touched. Dewey didn't play favorites; he loved everyone equally.

But even as I say that, I know it wasn't true. Dewey did have special relationships, and one I'll always remember was with Crystal. For decades the library had hosted a special Story Hour every week for local elementary and middle school special education classes. Before Dewey, the kids were poorly behaved. This was their big outing for the week, and they were excited: screaming, yelling, jumping up and down. But Dewey changed that. As they got to know him, the children learned that if they were too noisy or erratic, Dewey left. They would do anything to keep Dewey with them; after a few months, they became so calm you couldn't believe it was the same group of kids.

The children couldn't pet very well, since most were physically disabled. Dewey didn't care. As long as the children were somewhat quiet, Dewey spent the hour with them. He walked around the room and rubbed their legs. He jumped in their laps. The children became so fixated on him, they didn't notice anything else. If we had read them the phone book they couldn't have cared less.

Crystal was one of the more disabled members of the group. She was a beautiful girl of about eleven, but she had no speech and very little control of her limbs. She was in a wheelchair, and the wheelchair had a wooden tray on the front. When she came into the library, her head was always down and her eyes were staring at that tray. The teacher took off her coat or opened her jacket, and she didn't move. It was like she wasn't even there.

Dewey noticed Crystal right away, but they didn't form an immediate bond. She didn't seem interested in him, and there were plenty of children who desperately wanted his attention. Then one week Dewey jumped on Crystal's wheelchair tray. Crystal squealed. She had been coming to the library for years, and I didn't even know she could vocalize. That squeal was the first sound I ever heard her make.

Dewey started visiting Crystal every week. Every time he jumped onto her tray, Crystal squealed with delight. It was a loud, high-pitched squeal, but it never scared Dewey. He knew what it meant. He could feel her excitement, or maybe he could see the change in her face. Whenever she saw Dewey, Crystal glowed. Her eyes had always been blank. Now they were on fire.

Soon it wasn't just seeing Dewey on her tray. The moment the teacher pushed her into the library, Crystal was alive. When she saw Dewey, who waited for her at the front door, she immediately started to vocalize. It wasn't her usual high-pitched squeal but a deeper sound. I believed she was calling to Dewey. Dewey must have thought so, too, because as soon as he heard it, he was at her side. Once her wheelchair was parked, he jumped on her tray, and happiness exploded from within her. She started to squeal, and her smile, you couldn't believe how big and bright it was. Crystal had the best smile in the world.

Usually Crystal's teacher picked up her hand and helped her pet Dewey. That touch, the feel of his fur on her skin, always brought on a round of louder and more delighted squeals. I swear, one day she looked up and made eye contact with me. She was overcome with joy, and she wanted to share the moment with someone, with everyone. This from a girl who for years never lifted her eyes from the floor.

One week I picked Dewey off Crystal's tray and put him inside her coat. She didn't even squeal. She just stared down at him in awe. She was so happy. Dewey was so happy. He had a chest to lean on, and it was warm, and he was with somebody he loved. He wouldn't come out of her coat. He stayed in there for twenty minutes, maybe more. The other children checked out books. Dewey and Crystal sat together in front of the circulation desk. The bus was idling in front of the library, and all the other children were on it, but Dewey and Crystal were still sitting where we had left them, alone together. That smile, that moment, was worth the world.

I can't imagine Crystal's life. I don't know how she felt when she was out in the world, or even what she did. But I know that whenever she was in the Spencer Public Library with Dewey, she was happy. And I think she experienced the kind of complete happiness very few of us ever feel. Dewey knew that. He wanted her to experience that happiness, and he loved her for it. Isn't that a legacy worthy of any cat, or human being?

~

The list on the opposite page was written on a big orange piece of poster board and hung at the Spencer Public Library circulation desk for Dewey's first birthday, November 18, 1988.

DEWEY'S LIKES AND DISLIKES

Category	Loves	Hates
Food	Purina Special Dinners, Dairy Flavor!	Anything else
Place to sleep	Any box or someone's lap	Alone or in his own basket
Toy	Anything with catnip	Toys that don't move
Time of day	8 a.m. when the staff arrives	When everybody leaves
Body position	Stretched out on his back	Standing up for very long
Temperature	Warm, warm, warm	Cold, cold, cold
Hiding place	Between the Westerns on the bottom shelf	The lobby
Activity	Making new friends, watching the copier	Going to the vet
Petting	On the head, behind his ears	Scratched or touched on stomach
Equipment	Kim's typewriter, the copier	Vacuum cleaner
Animal	Himself!	
Grooming	Cleaning his ears	Being brushed or combed
Medicine	Felaxin (for hair balls)	Anything else
Game	Hide-and-seek, push the pen on the floor	Wrestling
People	Almost everyone	People who are mean to him
Noise	A snack being opened, paper rustling	Loud trucks, construction, dogs barking
Book	The Cat Who Would Be King	101 Uses for a Dead Cat

9

Dewey and Jodi

The relationship between Dewey and Crystal is important not just because it changed her life but because it illustrates something about Dewey. It shows his effect on people. His love. His understanding. The extent to which he cared. Take this one person, I'm saying every time I tell that story, multiply it by a thousand, and you'll begin to see how much Dewey meant to the town of Spencer. It wasn't everybody, but it was another person every day, one heart at a time. And one of those people, one very close to my own heart, was my daughter, Jodi.

I was a single mother, so when she was young Jodi and I were inseparable. We walked our cockapoo, Brandy. We went window-shopping at the mall. We had sleepovers in the living room, just the two of us. Whenever a movie came on television we wanted to see, we had a picnic on the floor. *The Wizard of Oz* – over the rainbow where everything is in color and you have the power to do what you've always wanted and that power has always been with you if only you knew how to tap into it – came on once a year, and it was our favorite. When Jodi was nine, we went every afternoon, weather permitting, to hike in a nearby wilderness area. At least once a week, we hiked all the way to the top of a limestone cliff, where we sat and looked down on the river, a mother and her daughter, talking together.

We lived in Mankato, Minnesota, but we spent a lot of time at my parents' house in Hartley, Iowa. For two hours, as the cornfields of Minnesota turned into the cornfields of Iowa, we sang along to the old eight-track, mostly corny 1970s songs by John Denver and Barry Manilow. And we always played a special game. I would say, 'Who's the biggest man you know?'

Jodi would answer, and then ask me, 'Who's the strongest woman you know?'

I would answer and ask, 'Who's the funniest woman you know?'

We asked questions back and forth until eventually I could think of only one more question, the one I had been waiting to ask. 'Who's the smartest woman you know?'

Jodi always answered, 'You, Mommy.' She had no idea how much I looked forward to hearing that.

Then Jodi turned ten. At ten, Jodi stopped answering the question. This behavior was typical of a girl that age, but I couldn't help being disappointed.

At thirteen, after we had moved to Spencer, she stopped letting me kiss her good night. 'I'm too old for that, Mommy,' she said one night.

'I know,' I told her. 'You're a big girl now.' But it broke my heart.

I remember walking out into the living room of our two-bedroom, 1,200-square-foot bungalow, which was only a mile from the library. Of course, half of Spencer was only a mile from the library. I looked out the window at the quiet, square houses on their nice square lawns. As in the rest of Iowa, most of the roads in Spencer were perfectly straight. Why wasn't life like that?

Brandy tottered up and nuzzled my hand. Brandy had been with me since I was pregnant with Jodi, and the dog was clearly feeling her age. She was lethargic, and for the first time in her life she was having accidents on the floor. Poor Brandy. Not you, too. I held out as long as I could, but eventually I took her to see Dr. Esterly, who diagnosed an advanced stage of kidney failure.

'She's fourteen years old. It's not unexpected.'

'What should we do?'

'I can treat it, Vicki, but there's no hope for recovery.'

I looked down at the poor, tired dog. She had always been there for me; she had given me everything. I took her head in my hands and scratched behind her ears. 'I can't afford much, girl, but I'll do what I can.'

Several weeks of pills later, I was sitting in my living room with Brandy on my lap when I felt something warm. Then I realized it was wet. Brandy was peeing all over me. I could tell she was not just embarrassed; she was in pain.

'It's time,' Dr. Esterly said.

I didn't tell Jodi, at least not everything. Partly to protect her. Partly because I didn't want to acknowledge it myself. I felt as if Brandy had been with me my whole life. I loved her; I needed her. I couldn't bring myself to put her down.

I called my sister, Val, and told her husband, Don, 'Please come by the house and pick her up. Don't tell me when, just do it.'

A few days later I came home for lunch and Brandy wasn't there. I knew what that meant. She was gone. I called Val and asked her to pick Jodi up from school and take her to dinner. I needed time to compose myself. At dinner Jodi could tell something was wrong. Eventually Val broke down and told her Brandy had been put to sleep.

I had done so many things wrong by this point. I had tried to treat Brandy's pain. I had left her to die with my brother-in-law. I hadn't been completely honest with Jodi. And I had allowed my sister to tell my daughter about the death of the dog she loved. But my biggest mistake was what I did when Jodi came home. I didn't cry. I didn't show any emotion. I told myself that I needed to be strong for her. I didn't want her to see how much I hurt. When Jodi went to school the next day, I broke down. I cried so hard I made myself sick. I was so distraught I couldn't even drive to work until the afternoon. But Jodi didn't see that. To her thirteen-year-old mind, I was the woman who killed her dog and didn't even care.

Brandy's death wasn't a turning point in our relationship. It was more a symptom of the gulf developing between us. Jodi wasn't a little child anymore, but part of me still treated her like one. She also wasn't an adult, but part of her thought she was all grown up and didn't need me any longer. Even as I realized, for the first time, the distance between us, Brandy's death pushed us further apart.

By the time Dewey arrived, Jodi was sixteen, and like many mothers of girls that age I felt we were living separate lives. Much of that was my fault. I was working very hard planning the library remodeling I had finally pushed through the city council, and I didn't have much time to spend at home. But it was her fault, too. Jodi spent most of her time out with friends or locked in her room. Most of the week, we interacted only at dinner. Even then we rarely had much to talk about.

Until Dewey. With Dewey, I had something to talk about that Jodi wanted to hear. I'd tell her what he did; who came to see him; whom he played with; what local newspaper or radio station called for an interview. A few staff members alternated feeding

Dewey on Sunday morning. Although I was never able to get Jodi out of bed for those Sunday-morning visits, we'd often drop by the library Sunday night on our way back from dinner at Mom and Dad's house.

You wouldn't believe Dewey's excitement when Jodi walked in that library door. The cat pranced. He would literally do flips off bookshelves just to impress her. While I was alone in the back room cleaning his litter and refilling his food dish, Dewey and Jodi played. She wasn't just another person spending time with him; Dewey was absolutely crazy for Jodi.

I've said Dewey never followed anyone around, that his style was to retain some distance, at least for a while. That wasn't true with Jodi. Dewey followed her like a dog. She was the only person in the world from whom he wanted and needed affection. Even when Jodi came to the library during work hours, Dewey sprinted to her side. He didn't care who saw him; he had no pride around that girl. As soon as she sat down, Dewey was in her lap.

On holidays, when the library was closed for a few days, I brought Dewey home with me. He didn't like the car ride – he always assumed it meant Dr. Esterly, so he spent the first couple minutes in the backseat on the floor – but as soon as he felt me turn off Grand Avenue onto Eleventh Street, he bounced up to stare out the window. As soon as I opened the door, he rushed into my house to give everything a nice long sniff. Then he ran up and down the basement stairs.

He lived in a one-floor world at the library, so he couldn't get enough of stairs.

Once he ran his excitement out on the stairs, Dewey would often settle in beside me on the sofa. Just as often, though, he sat on the back of the sofa and stared out the window. He was watching for Jodi. When she came home, he jumped right up and ran to the door. As soon as she walked in, Dewey was like Velcro. He never left Jodi's side. He got between her legs and almost tripped her, he was so excited. When Jodi took her shower, Dewey waited in the bathroom with her, staring at the curtain. If she closed the door, he sat right outside. If the shower stopped and she didn't come out quickly enough, he cried. As soon as she sat down, he was on her lap. It didn't matter if she was at the dinner table or on the toilet. He jumped on her, kneaded her stomach, and purred, purred, purred.

Jodi's room was an absolute mess. When it came to her appearance, the girl was immaculate. Not a hair out of place, not a speck of dirt anywhere. Put it this way: she ironed her socks. So who would believe her room looked like the lair of a troll? Only a teenager could live in a room where you couldn't see the floor or close the closet door, where crusty plates and glasses were buried under dirty clothes for weeks. I refused to clean it up, but I also refused to stop nagging her about it. A typical mother-daughter relationship, I know, but that's only easy to say after the fact. It's never easy when you're going through it.

But everything was easy for Dewey. Dirty room? Nagging mother? What did he care? *That's Jodi in there*, he said to me with one last look as he disappeared behind her door for the night. *What does that other stuff matter?*

Sometimes, just before turning in for the night, Jodi would call me to her room. I'd walk in and find Dewey guarding Jodi's pillow like a pot of gold or lying over the top half of her face. I'd look at him for a second, so desperate for her touch, and then we'd both start laughing. Jodi was silly and funny around her friends, but for all those high school years she was so serious with me. Dewey was the only thing that made our relationship lighthearted and playful. With Dewey around, we laughed together, almost like we had when Jodi was a child.

Jodi and I weren't the only ones Dewey was helping. Spencer Middle School was across the street from the library, and about fifty students were regularly staying with us after school. On the days they blew in like a hurricane, Dewey avoided them, especially the rowdy ones, but usually he was out mingling. He had many friends among the students, both boys and girls. They petted him and played games with him, like rolling pencils off the table and watching his surprise when they disappeared. One girl would wiggle a pen out the end of her coat sleeve. Dewey would chase the pen up the sleeve and then, deciding he liked that warm, dark place, he'd sometimes lie down for a nap.

Most of the kids left just after five when their parents got off work. A few stayed as late as eight. Spencer wasn't immune to problems – alcoholism, neglect, abuse – but our regulars were the children of blue-collar parents. They loved their kids but had to work extra jobs or extra shifts to make ends meet.

These parents, who came in for only a moment, rarely had time to pet Dewey. They worked long days, and they had meals to prepare and houses to clean before falling into bed. But their children spent hours with Dewey; he entertained and loved them. I never realized how much that meant, or how deep those bonds were, until I saw the mother of one of our boys bend down and whisper, 'Thank you, Dewey,' as she tenderly stroked his head.

I figured she was thanking him for spending time with her son, for filling up what could have been an awkward and lonely time for him.

She stood up and put her arm around her son. Then, as they were walking out the door, I heard her ask him, 'How was Dewey today?' Suddenly, I knew exactly how she felt. Dewey had turned a difficult time apart into common ground; he was her road back to so much of what she had left behind. I never considered this boy one of Dewey's close companions – he spent most of his time goofing off with friends or playing games on the computer – but clearly Dewey was having an impact on his life beyond the library walls. And it wasn't just this boy. The more I looked, the more I noticed that the ember that had ignited my relationship with Jodi was felt by other families, too. Like me, parents all over Spencer were spending their one hour a day with their teenagers talking about Dewey.

The staff didn't understand. They saw Jodi and Dewey together and thought I'd be offended that Dewey loved someone more than me. After Jodi left, someone would usually say, 'Her voice sounds just like yours. That's why he loves her so much.'

But I didn't feel jealous at all. Dewey and I had a complex relationship, one that involved baths, brushings, veterinary visits, and other unpleasant experiences. Dewey's relationship with Jodi was pure and innocent. It was fun and good times, uncomplicated by responsibility. If I wanted to put a Vicki spin on their relationship, I could say Dewey realized how important Jodi was to me, and that made her important to him. I could even stretch to say that maybe, just maybe, Dewey understood the significance of those moments the three of us shared, how much I missed laughing with my daughter, and he was therefore happy to throw himself over the chasm and serve as the bridge between us.

But I don't think that was it at all. Dewey loved Jodi because she was Jodi – warm, friendly, wonderful Jodi. And I loved him for loving my daughter.

10

A Long Way from Home

In Hartley, Iowa, where my family moved when I was fourteen, I was a straight arrow, the head student librarian, and the second smartest girl in my grade, after Karen Watts. It was all As for Vicki Jipson, except in typing, where I got a C. But that didn't keep me from having a reputation. One night I went with my parents to a dance in Sanborn, a little town nine miles from Hartley. When the dance hall closed at eleven, we went to the restaurant next door, where I promptly passed out. Dad took me outside for some fresh air, and I threw up. The next morning at eight thirty, my grandfather called the house and said, 'What the hell is going on over there? I heard Vicki was drunk in Sanborn last night.' The cause turned out to be an abscessed tooth, but there was no beating a bad reputation in a small town like Hartley.

My older brother, meanwhile, was considered one of the smartest kids ever to attend Hartley High School. Everyone called him the Professor. David graduated a year ahead of me and went to college a hundred miles away in Mankato, Minnesota. I figured I'd follow him there. When I mentioned my plans to my guidance counselor, he said, 'You don't need to worry about college. You're just going to get married, have kids, and let a man take care of you.' What a jerk. But it was 1966. This was rural Iowa. I didn't get any other advice.

After graduation from high school, I got engaged to the third boy I'd ever dated. We'd been going out for two years, and he adored me. But I needed to get away from the microscope of small-town Iowa; I needed to be out on my own. So I broke off the engagement, which was the hardest thing I'd ever done, and moved to Mankato with my best friend, Sharon.

While David went to college on the other side of town, Sharon and I worked at the Mankato Box Company. Mankato Box packaged products like Jet-Dry, the dishwashing liquid, and Gumby, who was a star at the time. I worked mostly on Punch and Grow, a container of potting soil with seeds attached to the lid. My job was to grab potting soil containers off a conveyor belt, snap on the plastic lid, slide them into a cardboard sleeve, and put them in a box. Sharon and I worked side by side, and we were always singing goofy lyrics about Punch and Grow to the tune of popular songs. We would get the whole line laughing, the Laverne and Shirley of Mankato Box. After three years, I worked my way up to feeding the empty plastic cups into the machine. The job was more isolated, so I didn't get to sing as much, but at least I didn't get filthy from all the potting soil.

Sharon and I developed a routine, which happens with line work. We would get off work exactly at five, ride the bus to our apartment for a quick dinner, then hit the dance clubs. We'd stay out, dancing our toes off, until they shut the dance halls down. If I wasn't dancing, I was usually out with my brother David and his friends. David was more than my brother, he was my best friend, and I can't count the number of times we stayed up talking about our lives. If I stayed home, which was rare, I'd put on a record and dance, all alone in my bedroom. I just had to dance. I loved to dance.

I met Wally Myron at a dance club, but he wasn't like the other guys I'd dated. He was very smart and very well-read, which impressed me immediately. And he had personality. Wally was always smiling, and everyone with him was always smiling, too. He was the kind of person who would go down to the corner store for milk and talk to the clerk for two hours. Wally could talk with anyone about anything.

He didn't have a mean bone in his body. I say it to this day: Wally was incapable of intentionally hurting anyone.

We dated for a year and a half before getting married in July 1970. I was twenty-two, and I got pregnant right away. It was a tough pregnancy, with sickness morning, noon, and night. Wally spent evenings after work out with his friends, usually riding motorcycles, but he was always home by seven thirty. He wanted a social wife, but he would take a sick wife if that meant a baby on the way.

Sometimes one decision changes your life, and it doesn't have to be one you make yourself – or even know about. When I went into labour, the doctor decided to speed the process with two massive doses of Pitocin. I found out later he had a party to attend, and he wanted to get this darn procedure over with. I went from three centimeters dilated to crowning in two hours. The shock broke my afterbirth, so they put me back into labor. They didn't get all the pieces. Six weeks later I hemorrhaged, and they rushed me back to the hospital for emergency surgery.

I had always wanted a daughter named Jodi Marie. I had dreamed about it from a young age. Now I had that daughter, Jodi Marie Myron, and I was dying to spend time with her, to hug her and talk to her and look into her eyes. But the surgery knocked me flat on my back. My hormones went haywire, and I was racked with headaches, insomnia, and cold sweats. Two years and six operations later my health hadn't improved, so my doctor suggested exploratory surgery. I woke up in the hospital bed to discover he'd taken both ovaries and my uterus. The physical pain was intense, but worse was the knowledge that I couldn't have any more children. I had expected a peek inside; I wasn't prepared to be hollowed out. And I wasn't prepared to enter sudden and severe menopause. I was twenty-four going on sixty, with scarring through my gut, regret in my heart, and a daughter I couldn't hold. The curtain came down and everything went black.

When I came around a few months later, Wally wasn't there. Not like he used to be, anyway. That's when I noticed, suddenly, that everything meant drinking to Wally. If he went fishing, it meant drinking. If he went hunting, it meant drinking. Even motorcycle riding meant drinking. Before long, he wasn't showing up when he promised. He would be out late and never call. He'd come home drunk, and I'd say, 'What are you doing? You have a sick wife and a two-year-old child!'

'We just went fishing,' he'd say. 'I had a couple too many. It's no big deal.'

I'd wake up the next morning and he'd be gone to work. I'd find a note on the kitchen table. *I love you. I don't want to fight. I'm sorry.* Wally could never sleep, and he would stay up all night writing me long letters. The man was smart. He could write beautifully. And every morning, when I saw those letters, I loved him.

The realization that your husband is a problem drinker comes suddenly, but the admission takes a long, long time. Your insides tie themselves in knots, but your heart refuses to understand. You make explanations, then excuses. You dread the ringing of the telephone. Then you dread the silence when it doesn't ring. Instead of talking, you throw out the beer. You pretend not to notice things, like money. He always comes through, but only when the cupboard is bare. But you're scared to complain. What are the chances, you think, that it will get worse instead of better?

'I understand,' he says when you mention it. 'It's not a problem. But I'll quit. For you. I promise.' But neither of you believes it.

Day by day, your world gets smaller. You don't want to open cabinets for fear of what you'll find. You don't want to search the pockets of his pants. You don't want to go anywhere. Where's he going to take you that doesn't involve drinking?

Many mornings I found beer bottles in the oven. Jodi found beer cans in her toy box. Wally was waking up early every morning, and if I dared to look out the window, I could see him sitting in his van drinking warm beer. He didn't even bother driving around the corner.

When Jodi was three, we went to Hartley for my brother Mike's wedding. Jodi and I were in the ceremony, so Wally had free time on his hands. He would disappear and not show up until late at night, when everyone was asleep.

'Are you trying to avoid us?' I asked him.

'No, I love your family. You know that.'

The family was sitting around Mom's kitchen table one night, and as usual Wally was nowhere to be found. We ran out of beer, so Mom went to the cabinet where she was keeping extra beer for all the friends and relatives in town. Most of it was gone.

'What were you thinking, taking Mom's beer?'

'I don't know. I'm sorry.'

'How do you think I feel? How do you think Jodi feels?'

'She doesn't know.'

'She's old enough to know. You just don't know her.'

Afraid to ask. Afraid not to ask. 'Are you even working?'

'Of course I am. You see the paychecks, don't you?'

Wally's father had given him part ownership of the family construction business, which meant Wally didn't get a steady paycheck. I couldn't tell if the company was between projects or if the whole world was crashing down around us.

'It's not just money, Wally.'

'I know. I'll spend more time at home.'

'Quit drinking for one week.'

'Why?'

'Wally.'

'Okay, one week. I'll quit.'

But again, neither of us believed it.

After Mike's wedding, I finally admitted to myself that Wally had a problem. That he was coming home less and less. That I almost never saw him sober. He wasn't a mean drunk, but he wasn't a functioning drunk, either. And yet he ran our lives. He drove our only car. I had to take the bus or ride with a friend to buy groceries. He cashed the paychecks. He paid the bills. Often I was too sick to follow the finances, much less raise a child on my own. I called our house the Blue Coffin because it was painted a hideous shade of blue and shaped like a casket. It started out as a joke – it was actually a fine house in a nice neighborhood – but within two years it felt like the truth. Jodi and I were stuck in that house, being buried alive.

My family came through for me. They never blamed me. They never lectured me. My parents didn't have money, but they took Jodi in, two weeks at a time, and raised her like their daughter. Whenever life smothered me, they gave me room to breathe.

Then there were my friends. If that delivery room doctor ruined my body, another stranger saved my mind. When Jodi was six months old, a woman knocked on my door. She had a daughter about Jodi's age in a stroller. She said, 'I'm Faith Landwer. My husband has been friends with your husband since high school, so let's have coffee and get to know each other.'

Thank goodness I agreed.

Faith got me involved in a newcomer's club that played cards once a month. I met Trudy over our regular game of Five Hundred, then met Barb, Pauli, Rita, and Idelle. Soon we were having coffee together at Trudy's house a couple days a week. We were all young mothers, and Trudy's house was the only one big enough to hold us. We would shove the children into her enormous playroom, sit at the kitchen table, and keep one another sane. I confided in them about Wally, and they didn't blink. Trudy just came around the table and gave me a hug.

What did my friends do for me in those years? What didn't they do for me? When I needed to run an errand, they drove me. When I was sick, they cared for me. When I needed someone to watch Jodi, they picked her up. I don't know how many times one of them dropped by with a plate of hot food just when I needed it.

'I just cooked a little extra casserole. Do you want it?'

And yet it wasn't my family or my friends who saved my life. Not really. My real motivation, my real reason for picking myself up every morning and struggling on, was my daughter, Jodi. She needed me to be her mother, to teach by example. We didn't have money, but we had each other. When I was confined to my bed, Jodi and I spent hours talking. When I was physically able, we walked in the park with the real third member of our family. Brandy and Jodi looked up to me; they adored me without question or doubt; they gave me unconditional love, which is the secret power of children and dogs. Every night when I put Jodi to bed, I kissed her, and that touch, that skin on my skin, sustained me.

'I love you, Mom.'

'I love you, too. Good night.'

A hero of mine, Dr. Charlene Bell, says everyone has a pain thermometer that goes from zero to ten. No one will make a change until they reach ten. Nine won't do it. At nine, you are still afraid. Only ten will move you, and when you're there, you'll know. No one can make that decision for you.

I saw that firsthand with one of my friends. She was pregnant, and her abusive husband was still beating her every day. We decided we had to get her out of there before it was too late, so we talked her into leaving him. We set her up in a trailer with her kids. Her parents came by every day. She had everything she needed. Two weeks later she went back to her husband. I realized then you can't make people do what you know is right. They have to come to it on their own. A year later my friend left her husband for good. She didn't need help from any of us.

I learned that lesson for myself, too, because a marriage unwraps slowly. Maybe it's not the slowness but the consistency that crushes you. Every day is a little bit worse, a little less predictable, until finally you're doing things you never, ever thought you'd do. I was looking for food in the kitchen one night, and I found a checkbook. It was for a secret banking account Wally had set up for himself. I turned on the grill at two in the morning, ripped out the checks one by one, and burned them. Halfway through I thought, 'Sane people don't live like this.'

But I stayed. I was worn out. I was emotionally drained. My confidence was crippled. I was physically weak from the surgeries. And I was scared. But not scared enough to make a change.

The last year was the worst. It was so bad, I can't even remember the details. The whole year was black. Wally had stopped coming home before three in the morning, and since we were sleeping in different rooms, I never saw him. He left the house early every morning, but I didn't know where he went. He had been pushed out of the family business, and our money situation was drifting from bad to unbearable. Mom and Dad sent me what they could. Then they went to the rest of the family and collected several hundred dollars more. When that ran out, Jodi and I had nothing to eat. We lived on oatmeal, nothing but oatmeal, for two weeks. I finally went to Wally's mother, who I knew blamed me for her son's condition.

'Don't do it for me,' I said. 'Do it for your granddaughter.' She bought one bag of groceries, set it on the kitchen table, and left.

A few nights later Wally came home. Jodi was asleep. I was in the living room reading *One Day at a Time*, the bible of Al-Anon, a support group for people affected by alcoholics. I didn't yell or hit him or anything like that. We both acted as if Wally came home all the time. I hadn't seen him in a year, and I was surprised how bad he looked. He was thin. He was sickly. He clearly wasn't eating. I could smell alcohol, and he still had the shakes. He sat down on the other side of the room without a word, this man who used to talk for hours to anyone, and watched me read. Eventually he dozed off, so it surprised me when he said, 'What are you smiling about?'

'Nothing,' I told him, but when he asked I knew. I had reached ten. No fireworks. No final injustice. The moment had slipped in as quiet as a stranger coming home.

I went to a lawyer the next day and started divorce proceedings. That's when I discovered we were six months behind on house payments, six months behind on car payments, and $6,000 in debt. Wally had even taken out a home-improvement loan, but of course no work had been done. The Blue Coffin was falling apart.

Grandma Stephenson – Mom's mother, who had divorced her own alcoholic husband – gave me the money to save the house. We let the bank repossess the car. It wasn't worth saving. My dad passed the hat in Hartley and came up with $800 to buy me a 1962 Chevy an old lady didn't even drive in the rain. I had never driven a car in my life. I took driving lessons for a month and passed my driver's test. I was twenty-eight years old.

The first place I drove that car was to the welfare office. I had a six-year-old daughter, a high school diploma, a medical history that can only be called a disaster, and a pile of debt. I didn't have a choice. I told them, 'I need help, but I'm only going to take it if you let me go to college.'

Thank goodness welfare was different in those days. They agreed. I went straight to Mankato State and registered for the upcoming semester. Four years later, in 1981, I graduated summa cum laude, the highest level of honors, with a general studies degree, double majors in psychology and women's studies, and minors in anthropology and library science. Welfare paid for the whole thing: classes, housing, living expenses. My brothers David and Mike had dropped out without graduating, and so, at the age of thirty-two, I became the first Jipson to earn a diploma from a four-year college. Twelve years later Jodi would become the second.

11

Hide-and-Seek

After graduation I found out it takes more than a college degree to become a psychologist. To make ends meet, I took a job as a secretary for my friend Trudy's husband, Brian. After a week, I told him, 'Don't waste any more money training me. I'm not going to stay.' I hated filing. I hated typing. After thirty-two years, I was tired of taking orders. For most of my adult life I had tried to be the person my guidance counselor predicted I'd be way back at Hartley High School. I had followed the path set out for me and just about every other woman of my generation. I didn't want to do that anymore.

My sister, Val, who lived in Spencer, mentioned an opening at the local library. At that moment I had no intention of returning home. Despite my minor in library science, I had never really considered working in a library. But I took the interview, and I loved the people. A week later, I was on my way back to northwest Iowa, the new assistant director of the Spencer Public Library.

I wasn't expecting to love the job. Like most people, I thought being a librarian meant stamping due dates in the back of books. But it was so much more. Within months, I was neck-deep in marketing campaigns and graphic design. I started a homebound program, which took books to people unable to visit the library, and developed a major initiative to interest teens in reading. I developed programs for nursing homes and schools; I started answering questions on the radio and speaking to social clubs and community organizations. I was a big-picture person, and I was beginning to see the difference a strong library made in a community. Then I got involved in the business side of running a library – the budgeting and long-range planning – and I was hooked. This was a job, I realized, I could love for the rest of my life.

In 1987, my friend and boss, Bonnie Pluemer, was promoted to a regional library management position. I spoke confidentially to several members of the library board and told them I wanted to be the new director. Unlike the rest of the applicants, who interviewed at the library, I interviewed secretly at a board member's house. After all, a small town can turn quickly from nurturing nest to nettle bush when it looks like you're getting too big for your britches.

Most of the members of the library board were fond of me but skeptical. They kept asking me, 'Are you sure you can *handle* this job?'

'I've been assistant director for five years, so I know the position better than anyone. I know the staff. I know the community. I know the library's problems. The last three directors have moved on to regional positions. Do you really want another person who views this job as a stepping-stone?'

'No, but do you really *want* the job?'

'You have no idea how much I want this job.'

Life is a journey. After all I'd been through, it was inconceivable this wasn't my next step, or that I wasn't the best person for the job. I was older than past directors. I had a daughter. I wasn't going to take an opportunity lightly.

'This is my place,' I told the board. 'There's nowhere else I want be.'

The next day they offered me the position.

I wasn't qualified. That's not an opinion, it's a fact. I was smart, experienced, and hardworking, but the job required a master's degree in library science and I didn't have one. The board was willing to overlook this fact as long as I started a master's program within two years. That seemed more than fair, so I accepted the offer.

Then I found out the nearest American Library Association–accredited master's program was five hours away in Iowa City. I was a single mother. I had a full-time job. That wasn't going to work.

Today you can earn an accredited master's degree in library science on the Internet. But in 1987 I couldn't even find a long-distance learning program. And believe me, I looked. Finally, at the urging of my regional administrator, John Houlahan, Emporia State University in Emporia, Kansas, took the plunge. The first American Library Association–accredited long-distance master's program in the nation met in Sioux City, Iowa, in the fall of 1988. And I was the first student in the door.

I loved the classes. This wasn't cataloging and checking out books. This was demographics; psychology; budgeting and business analysis; the methodology of information processing. We learned community relations. We spent twelve grueling weeks on community analysis, which is the art of figuring out what patrons want. On the surface, community analysis is easy. In Spencer, for instance, we didn't carry books on snow skiing, but we always had the latest information on fishing and boating because the lakes were only twenty minutes away.

A good librarian, though, digs deeper. What does your community value? Where has it been? How and why has it changed? And most important, where is it going? A good librarian develops a filter in the back of her brain to catch and process information. Farm crisis in full swing? Don't just stock up on résumé builders and career manuals; purchase books on engine repair and other cost-saving measures. Hospital hiring nurses? Update the medical manuals and partner with the local community college to help them utilize your resources. More women working outside the home? Start a second Story Hour in the evening and concentrate on day-care centers during the day.

The material was complex, the homework brutal. All the students were working librarians, and there were several other single mothers. This program wasn't a casual decision; it was a last chance, and we were willing to work for it. In addition to attending class from five thirty on Friday to noon on Sunday – after a two-hour drive to Sioux City, no less – we were researching and writing two papers a week, sometimes more. I didn't have a typewriter at home, much less a computer, so I would leave work at five, cook dinner for myself and Jodi, then head back to the library and work until midnight or later.

At the same time I threw myself into the library remodeling. I wanted to complete it by the summer of 1989, and I had months of work to do before we could even begin. I learned space planning, section organization, disability compliance. I chose colors, mapped furniture arrangements, and decided whether there was enough money for new tables and chairs (there wasn't, so we refurbished the old ones). Jean Hollis Clark and I made exact scale models of the old library and the new library to display on the circulation desk. It wasn't enough to plan a great remodel; the public had to be enthusiastic and informed. Dewey helped out by sleeping every day inside one of the models.

Once a design was determined, I moved on to the next step: planning how to move more than 30,000 objects out of the building, then put them all back into their correct places. I found warehouse space. I found moving equipment. I organized and scheduled volunteers. And every plan, every penny, had to be tallied and earmarked and justified to the library board.

The hours at work and in class were wearing me down, physically and mentally, and the school fees were straining my budget. So I could hardly believe it when the city council started an employee education fund. If city employees went back to school to enhance their job performance, the town would pay for it. Donna Fisher, the city clerk, received a well-deserved degree. When I mentioned my master's program at a city council meeting, the reception wasn't as accommodating.

Cleber Meyer, our new mayor, was sitting opposite me at the end of the table. Cleber was the epitome of a Sister's Café power broker, a blue-collar, salt-of-the-earth type. He had only an eighth-grade education, but he had a loud voice, broad shoulders, and his finger on the pulse of Spencer. Cleber owned and operated a gas station, Meyer Service Station, but you could tell from his huge rough hands that he grew up on the farms. In fact, he grew up outside

Moneta; he and Dad had known each other all their lives. And yes, Cleber was his real name. His brother's name, if you can believe it, was Cletus.

For all his bluster, Cleber Meyer was the finest man you will ever meet. He would lend you the shirt off his back (gas stains included), and I don't believe he had it in him to hurt anyone. He meant well, and he always had the best interest of Spencer at heart. But he was a 'good ole boy', he was opinionated, and let's just say he could be gruff. When I mentioned my master's program, Cleber slammed his fist on the table and thundered, 'Who do you think you are? A city employee?'

David Scott, a local attorney and council member, cornered me a few days later and said he'd go to bat for my expenses. After all, I *was* a city employee.

'Don't bother,' I told him. 'It will only hurt the library.' I had no intention of undoing all the goodwill Dewey had begun to foster.

Instead, I worked harder. More hours on schoolwork: writing, researching, studying. More work on the remodeling project: planning, researching, budgeting. More work running the day-to-day operations of the library. All of which meant, unfortunately, less time with my daughter. One Sunday Val's phone call caught me just as I was leaving Sioux City.

'Hi, Vicki. I hate to tell you this, but last night . . .'

'What happened? Where's Jodi?'

'Jodi's fine. But your house . . .'

'Yes?'

'Look, Vicki, Jodi had a party for a few friends and, well, it got a little out of control.' She paused. 'Just imagine the worst for the next two hours and you'll be happy with what you find.'

The house was a wreck. Jodi and her friends had spent the morning cleaning, but there were still stains on the carpet . . . and ceiling. The vanity door in the bathroom was ripped off its hinges. The kids threw all my records against the wall and broke them. Someone put beer cans down the heating vents. My pills were gone. A depressed kid had locked himself in the bathroom and tried to overdose – on estrogen. I found out later the police were called twice, but since the football team was at the party and since it was a winning season, they looked the other way. The mess didn't bother me, not really, but it reminded me once again that Jodi was growing up without me. The only thing I couldn't whip with more work, I realized, was my relationship with my daughter.

Ironically it was Cleber Meyer who put it all in perspective. He was pumping gas for me at his station one day – yes, he was the mayor, but it was a part-time position – when the subject of Jodi came up. 'Don't worry,' he told me. 'When they turn fifteen, you become the dumbest person in the world. But when they turn twenty-two, you get smart again.'

Work, school, home life, petty local politics, I did what I always did in times of stress: I took a deep breath, dug inside, and forced myself to stand up taller than ever before. I had been picking myself up by my bootstraps all my life. There wasn't anything about this situation, I told myself, that I couldn't handle. It was only late at night in the library, alone with my thoughts and staring at that blank computer screen, that I began to feel the pressure. It was only then, in my first quiet moment of the day, that I felt my foundation begin to shake.

A library after closing is a lonely place. It is heart-poundingly silent, and the rows of shelves create an almost unfathomable number of dark and creepy corners. Most of the librarians I know won't stay alone in a library after closing, especially after dark, but I was never nervous or scared. I was strong. I was stubborn. And most of all, I was never alone. I had Dewey. Every night, he sat on top of the computer screen as I worked, lazily swiping his tail back and forth. When I hit a wall, either from writer's block, fatigue, or stress, he jumped down into my lap or onto the keyboard. *No more*, he told me. *Let's play*. Dewey had an amazing sense of timing.

'All right, Dewey,' I told him. 'You go first.'

Dewey's game was hide-and-seek, so as soon as I gave the word he would take off around the corner into the main part of the library. Half the time I immediately spotted the back half of a long-haired orange cat. For Dewey, hiding meant sticking your head in a bookshelf; he seemed to forget he had a tail.

'I wonder where Dewey is,' I said out loud as I snuck up on him. 'Boo!' I yelled when I got within a few feet, sending Dewey running.

Other times he was better hidden. I would sneak around a few shelves with no luck, then turn the corner to see him prancing toward me with that big Dewey smile.

You couldn't find me! You couldn't find me!

'That's not fair, Dewey. You only gave me twenty seconds.'

Occasionally he curled up in a tight spot and stayed put. I'd look for five minutes, then start calling his name. 'Dewey! Dewey!' A dark library can feel empty when you're bending over between the stacks and looking through rows of books, but I always imagined Dewey somewhere, just a few feet away, laughing at me.

'All right, Dewey, that's enough. You win!' Nothing. Where could that cat be? I'd turn around and there he was, standing in the middle of the aisle, staring at me.

'Oh, Dewey, you clever boy. Now it's my turn.'

I'd run and hide behind a bookshelf, and invariably one of two things happened. I'd get to my hiding place, turn around, and Dewey would be standing right there. He had followed me.

Found you. That was easy.

His other favorite thing to do was run around the other side of the shelf and beat me to my hiding spot.

Oh, is this where you're thinking about hiding? Because, well, I've already figured it out.

I'd laugh and pet him behind the ears. 'Fine, Dewey. Let's just run for a while.'

We'd run between the shelves, meeting at the end of the aisles, nobody quite hiding and no one really seeking. After fifteen minutes I would completely forget my research paper, or the most recent budget meeting for the remodeling project, or that unfortunate conversation with Jodi. Whatever had been bothering me, it was gone. The weight, as they say, was lifted.

'Okay, Dewey. Let's get back to work.'

Dewey never complained. I'd climb back into my chair, and he'd climb back to his perch on top of the computer and start waving his tail in front of the screen. The next time I needed him, he'd be there.

It's not a stretch to say those games of hide-and-seek with Dewey, that time spent together, got me through. Maybe it would be easier, right now, to tell you Dewey put his head on my lap and whimpered while I cried or that he licked the tears from my face. Anyone can relate to that. And it is almost true, because sometimes when the ceiling started falling in on me and I found myself staring blankly down at my lap, tears in my eyes, Dewey was there, right where I needed him to be.

But life isn't neat and tidy. Our relationship can't be tied up with a few tears. I'm not much of a crier, for one thing. And while Dewey was demonstrative with his love – he was always a soft touch for a late-night cuddle – he didn't bathe me with affection. Somehow Dewey knew when I needed a little nudge or a warm body, and he knew when the best thing for me was a stupid, mindless game of hide-and-seek. And whatever I needed, he'd give me, without thought, without wanting something in return, and without me asking. It wasn't just love. It was more than that. It was respect. It was empathy. And it went both ways. That spark Dewey and I had felt when we met? Those nights alone together in the library turned it into a fire.

I guess my final answer is that when everything in my life was so complex, when things were sliding in so many directions at once and it seemed at times the center wouldn't hold, my relationship with Dewey was so simple, and so natural, and that's what made it so right.

12

Christmas

Christmas is a holiday the town of Spencer celebrates together. It's the slow season for the farmers and manufacturers, a time to relax and spread our collected coins around to the merchants. The activity of the season is the Grand Meander, a walking tour of Grand Avenue that begins the first weekend in December. The whole street is strung with white lights, a coordinated display that shows off the fine lines of our buildings. Christmas music is piped in; Santa Claus comes out to receive wish lists from the children. His elves, also in Santa suits, ring bells on corners and collect coins for charities. The whole town is out, laughing, talking, clutching one another to share the warmth. The stores stay open late, showing off their holiday selections and offering cookies and hot chocolate to fight off the biting cold.

Every storefront window is decorated. We call them Living Windows, because in each one local residents act out holiday scenes. The Parker Museum, which houses a collection of Clay County artifacts, including a fire truck that battled the great fire of 1931, always creates a variation on the pioneers' Christmas. Other windows offer interpretations of Christmases not quite so long past, with Radio Flyers and porcelain dolls. Some have mangers. Others feature toy tractors and cars, a boy's view of Christmas morning. You can't look at the windows, playful or touching, funny or serious, and not think of the hundred and fifty previous meanders up and down this stretch of stores, and the next hundred and fifty to come. This, the windows all say, is Spencer.

The Festival of Trees, a Christmas-tree decorating contest, is held on the corner of First Avenue and Fifth Street, inside what used to be the Spencer Convention Center but is now the Eagles Club, a military-related social club that holds dances and dinners to raise money for charity. Since 1988 was Dewey's first Christmas, the library entered a tree under the title Do-We Love Christmas? The tree was decorated with – what else? – pictures of Dewey. It also featured puffy kitten ornaments and garlands of red yarn. The presents under the tree were appropriate books, like

The Cat-a-log and *The Cat in the Hat,* tied in neat red bows. Visitors could wander through the trees for a small charitable donation. There was no official judging, but I don't think it's a stretch to say Do-We Love Christmas? was the winner, hands down.

Christmas at the library, like Christmas on Grand Avenue, was a time to put away other concerns and focus on the here and now. After a stressful fall, I was happy to stop thinking about school and remodeling and, for a change, focus on decorations. The Monday after the Grand Meander, we took the boxes down from the top shelves of the storage room to prepare for the holiday season. The centerpiece was our big artificial Christmas tree next to the circulation desk. The first Monday in December, Cynthia Behrends and I always arrived early to set up and decorate the tree. Cynthia was the hardest worker on staff and eagerly volunteered for every job. But she didn't know what she was getting into because this year, when we slid the long thin Christmas tree box off its high shelf, we had company.

'Dewey's excited this morning. He must like the looks of this box.'

'Or the smell of all that plastic.' I could see his nose sniffing ninety odors a minute and his mind racing. *Could it be? All this time, could Mom have been hiding the world's largest, most spectacular, most deliciously smelly rubber band?*

When we pulled the Christmas tree out of the box, I could almost see Dewey's jaw drop.

It's not a rubber band, it's . . . it's . . . better.

As we pulled each branch out of the box, Dewey lunged at it. He wanted to sniff and chew every green piece of plastic sticking out of every green wire branch. He pulled a few plastic needles off the tree and started working them around in his mouth.

'Give me those, Dewey!'

He coughed a few pieces of plastic onto the floor. Then he leaped forward and thrust his head into the box just as Cynthia was pulling out the next branch.

'Back off, Dewey.'

Cynthia pulled him out, but a second later he was back, a green needle stuck to the moist tip of his nose. This time, his whole head disappeared inside the box. 'This isn't going to work, Dewey. Do you want me to get the rest of the tree out or not?'

Apparently the answer was not, because Dewey wasn't moving.

'All right, Dewey, out you go. I'd hate for you to lose an eye.' Cynthia wasn't scolding him, she was laughing. Dewey got the message and jumped back, only to start burrowing into the pile of branches on the floor.

'This is going to take all day,' Cynthia said.

'I sure hope so.'

As Cynthia pulled the last branches out of the box, I started to assemble the tree. Dewey was prancing and grinning, watching my every move. He came in for a sniff and a taste, then bounced back a few feet for perspective. The poor cat looked like he was about to explode with excitement. *Hurry up, hurry up. I want my turn.* This was the happiest I'd seen him all year.

'Oh, no, Dewey, not again.'

I looked over to find Dewey buried in the Christmas tree box, no doubt sniffing and pawing at the scents clinging to the cardboard. He disappeared completely inside, and a few seconds later the box was rolling back and forth across the floor. He stopped, poked his head out, and looked around. He spotted the half-assembled tree and bolted back to chew on the lower branches.

'I think he's found a new toy.'

'I think he's found a new *love*,' I said as I put the top branches into the notches on the green pole that comprised the trunk of our tree.

It was true. Dewey loved the Christmas tree. He loved the smell of it. The feel of it. The taste of it. Once I had it assembled and set up next to the circulation desk, he loved to sit under it. *Mine now,* he said as he rounded the base a few times. *Just leave us be, thanks.*

'Sorry, Dewey. Still work to do. We don't even have it decorated yet.'

Out came the ornaments, the new tinsel in this year's color, the pictures and special embellishments for this year's theme. Angels on strings. Santa Clauses. Shiny balls with glitter all over them. Ribbons, ornaments, cards, and dolls. Dewey rushed up to each box, but he had little interest in cloth and metal, hooks and lights. He was distracted by our wreath, which I had

made out of worn-out pieces of the library's previous
Christmas tree, but old plastic was no match for the
new, shiny stuff. Soon it was back to his spot under
the tree.

We started hanging ornaments. One minute Dewey
was in the boxes, finding out which ornaments came
next. The next minute he was at our feet, playing with
our shoelaces. Then he was stretching into the tree
for another whiff of plastic. A few seconds later he
was gone.

'What's that rustling sound?'

Suddenly Dewey came tearing by us with his head
through the strap of one of the plastic grocery bags
we used for storage. He ran all the way to the far side
of the library, then came careening back toward us.

'Catch him!'

Dewey dodged and kept running. Soon he was on
his way back again. Cynthia blocked the area near the
front door. I took the circulation desk. Dewey sprinted
right between us. I could see from the look in his eyes
he was in a frenzy. He had no idea how to get the
plastic bag from around his neck. His only thought
was, *Keep running. Maybe I can lose this monster.*

Soon there were four or five of us chasing him,
but he wouldn't stop dodging and sprinting away. It
didn't help that we were all laughing at him.

'Sorry, Dewey, but you've got to admit this is
funny.'

I finally cornered him and, despite his terrified
squirming, managed to free him from the bag.

Dewey immediately went over to his new best friend, the Christmas tree, and lay down under the branches for a nice, comforting tongue bath, complete with his customary fist in the ears. There would be a hair ball, no doubt, either later today or tomorrow morning. But at least one lesson had been learned. From then on, Dewey hated plastic bags.

That first day with the library Christmas tree was one of our best. The staff spent the entire day laughing, and Dewey spent the entire day – plastic bag run excluded, of course – in a state of gooey, romantic bliss. His love for the Christmas tree never diminished. Every year when the box came off the shelf, he pranced.

The librarians usually received a few gifts from grateful patrons, but that year our small trove of chocolates and cookies was dwarfed by Dewey's enormous stack of balls, treats, and toy mice. It seemed that everyone in town wanted Dewey – and us – to know just how much he meant to them. There were some fancy toys in that stash, even some nice homemade items, but Dewey's favorite toy from that holiday season wasn't a gift at all; it was a skein of red yarn he found in a decorating box. That yarn skein was Dewey's constant companion, not just for the holiday season but for years to come. He batted it around the library until a few feet of yarn stuck out, which he then pounced on, wrestled, and, very soon, got wrapped around his body. More than once, I was almost run down by an orange cat streaking across the staff area, red yarn in mouth, dragging the bundle behind him. An hour later he'd be sacked out under the Christmas tree, all four feet clutching his red buddy.

The library was closed for a few days at Christmas, so Dewey came home with me. He spent much of his time alone, though, because Christmas in Hartley was a Jipson family tradition. Everyone came to Mom and Dad's house for Christmas; you might be disowned if you didn't. You weren't allowed to miss any of the holiday activities, and there were a lot of them: extravagant meals; decorating parties; games for children; holiday carols; desserts and cookies; games for adults; relatives dropping by with a plate of cookies or nothing much, just a little something I saw in Sioux City and thought you'd love; a year's worth of stories, told and retold. There was always a story to tell around the family tree. The presents weren't extravagant, but every Jipson got to spend a week in the arms of a large extended family, and that's the best gift of all.

Eventually someone always said, 'Let's play "Johnny M'Go."'

Mom and Dad collected antiques, and a few years earlier we'd used them to form the Jipson family band. I played bass, which was a washtub with a broom handle attached to the top and a string running between them. My sister played the washboard. Dad and Jodi banged out a rhythm with a couple of spoons. Mike blew on a comb covered with wax paper. Doug blew across the mouth of a moonshine jar. It was an antique jar, of course, never used for its intended purpose. Mom turned an old pioneer-era wooden butter churn upside down and played it like a drum. Our song was 'Johnny B. Goode.' When she was little, Jodi always said, 'Play "Johnny M'Go"!' The name stuck. Every year we played 'Johnny M'Go' and other old rock-and-roll songs deep into the night on our homemade instruments, a homage to a country tradition that probably never existed in this part of Iowa, laughing with one another the whole time.

After Midnight Mass on Christmas Eve, Jodi and I headed home to Dewey, who as always was eager to see us. We spent Christmas morning together in Spencer, just the three of us. I hadn't even gotten Dewey a present. What would be the point? He already had more stuff than he needed. And after a year together, our relationship had gone well beyond token gifts and forced attention. We didn't have anything to prove. All Dewey wanted or expected from me was a few hours a day of my time. I felt the same way. That afternoon I dropped Jodi at Mom and Dad's house and slipped home to spend time with Dewey on the couch, doing nothing, saying nothing, just two friends lounging around like a couple of old socks waiting for a shoe.

13

A Great Library

A great library doesn't have to be big or beautiful. It doesn't have to have the best facilities or the most efficient staff or the most users. A great library provides. It is enmeshed in the life of a community in a way that makes it indispensable. A great library is one nobody notices because it is always there, and it always has what people need.

The Spencer Public Library was founded in 1883 in Mrs. H.C. Crary's parlor. In 1890, the library moved to a small frame building on Grand Avenue. In 1902, Andrew Carnegie granted the town $10,000 for a new library. Carnegie was a product of the industrial revolution that had turned a nation of farmers into factory workers, oilmen, and iron smelters. He was a ruthless corporate capitalist who built his United States Steel into the nation's most successful business. He was also a Baptist, and by 1902 he was deep into the pursuit of giving away his money to worthwhile causes. One cause was providing grants to small towns for libraries. For a town like Spencer, a Carnegie library was a sign you had made it not exactly to the top, but farther than Hartley and Everly.

The Spencer Public Library opened on March 6, 1905, on East Third Street, half a block off Grand Avenue. It was typical of Carnegie libraries, since Carnegie had mandated a classical style and symmetry of design. There were three stained-glass windows in the entrance hall, two with flowers and one with the word *library*. The librarian perched behind a large central desk, surrounded by drawers of cards. The side rooms were small and cloistered, with bookshelves to the ceiling. In an era when public buildings were segregated by sex, men and women were free to enter any room. Carnegie libraries were also among the first to let patrons choose books off the shelves instead of making requests to the librarian.

Some historians describe Carnegie libraries as plain, but that is true only in comparison to the elaborate central libraries of cities like New York and Chicago, which had carved friezes, ornately painted ceilings, and crystal chandeliers. Compared to the parlor of a local woman's home or a storefront on Grand Avenue, the Spencer Carnegie library was impossibly ornate. The ceiling was high, the windows enormous. The half-underground bottom floor held the children's library, an innovation at a time when children were often kept locked away in their homes. Children could sit and read on a circular bench, while above them a window looked out at ground level on a flat grass lawn. The floorboards throughout the building were dark wood, highly polished and very wide. They creaked when you walked, and often that creaking was the only sound you could hear. The Carnegie was a library where books were seen, not heard. It was a museum. It was as quiet as a church. Or a monastery. It was a shrine to learning, and in 1902 learning meant books.

When many people think of a library, they think of a Carnegie library. These are the libraries of our childhood. The quiet. The high ceilings. The central library desk, complete with matronly librarian (at least in our memories). These libraries seemed designed to make children believe you could get lost in them, and nobody could ever find you, and it would be the most wonderful thing.

By the time I was hired in 1982, the old Carnegie library was gone. It had been beautiful but small. Too small for a growing town. The land deed specified the town must use it for a library or return it to the owner, so in 1971 the town tore down the old Carnegie building to build a bigger, more modern, more efficient library, one without squeaky floorboards, dim lighting, imposingly high bookshelves, and rooms to get lost in.

It was a disaster.

Spencer is built in a traditional style. The retail buildings are brick, the houses along Third Street two- and three-story frame boardinghouses. The new library was concrete. One story tall, it hunched on the corner like a bunker. Its original wide lawn was gone, replaced by two tiny gardens. Too shadowed to grow much, they were soon filled in with rocks. The glass front doors were set back from the street, but the entryway was enclosed and unwelcoming. The east wall, which faced the town middle school, was solid concrete. Grace Renzig lobbied herself onto the library board in the late 1970s with the goal of having vines planted along the east wall. She got her vines a few years later, but she ended up staying on the board for almost twenty years.

The new Spencer Public Library was modern, but with a brutish efficiency. And it was flat-out cold. A glass wall faced north, with a lovely view of the alley. In the winter, you couldn't keep the back of the library warm. The floor plan was open, leaving no space for storage. There was no designated staff area. There were only five electric outlets. The furniture, made by local craftsmen, was beautiful but impractical. The tables had prominent support bars so you couldn't pull up additional chairs, and they were solid oak with black laminate tops, so they were too heavy to move. The carpet was orange, a Halloween nightmare.

Or to put it more simply, the building wasn't right for a town like Spencer. The library had always been well run. The collection of books was exceptional, especially for a town the size of Spencer, and the directors had always been early adopters of new technologies and ideas. For enthusiasm, professionalism, and expertise, the library was top-notch. But after 1971, it was all squeezed into the wrong building. The exterior didn't fit the surrounding area. The interior wasn't practical or friendly. It didn't make you want to sit down and relax. It was cold in every sense of the word.

We started the remodel – let's call it the warming process – in May 1989, just as northwest Iowa was waking up and changing from brown to green. The lawns suddenly needed mowing, the trees on Grand Avenue were throwing out new leaves. On the farms, the plants were pushing through the soil and unfolding, and you could finally see the result of all that time spent fixing equipment, churning fields, and planting seeds. The weather turned warm. The kids brought out bicycles. At the library, after almost a year of planning, it was finally time to work.

The first stage of remodeling was painting the bare concrete walls. We decided to leave the nine-foot bookshelves bolted to the walls, so Tony Joy, our painter and the husband of staff member Sharon Joy, simply had to throw on some drop cloths and lean his ladder against the shelves. But as soon as he did, Dewey climbed up.

'All right, Dewey, down we go.'

Dewey wasn't paying attention. He'd been in the library more than a year, but he'd never seen it from nine feet up. It was a revelation. Dewey stepped off the ladder and onto the top of the wall shelf. With a few steps, he was out of reach.

Tony moved the ladder. Dewey moved again. Tony climbed to the top, propped his elbow on the bookshelf, and looked at this stubborn cat.

'This is a bad idea, Dewey. I'm going to paint this wall, then you're going to rub against it. Vicki's going to see a blue cat, and then you know what's going to happen? I'm going to get fired.' Dewey just stared down at the library. 'You don't care, do you? Well, I warned you. Vicki!'

'Right here.'

'You've been watching?'

'It's a fair warning. I won't hold you responsible.'

I wasn't worried about Dewey. He was the most conscientious cat I'd ever known. He raced down bookshelves without a misstep. He intentionally brushed displays with his side, as cats do, without knocking them over. I knew he could not only walk a shelf without touching wet paint, but also tiptoe up a ladder without knocking off the can of paint at the top. I was more worried about Tony. It's not easy sharing a ladder with the king of the library.

'I'm fine with the arrangement if you are,' I called up to him.

'I'll take my chances,' Tony joked.

Within a few days, Tony and Dewey were fast friends. Or maybe I should say Tony and Dewkster, because that's what Tony always called him. Tony felt Dewey was too soft a name for such a macho cat. He worried the local alley cats were congregating outside the children's library window at night to make fun of his name. So Tony decided his real name wasn't Dewey, it was the Duke, like John Wayne. 'Only his close friends call him Dewkster,' Tony explained. He always called me Madame President.

'What do you think of this shade of red, Madame President?' he would ask when he saw me crossing the library.

'I don't know. It looks pink to me.'

But pink paint wasn't our biggest worry. Suddenly we couldn't keep our polite, well-behaved cat off the top of the wall shelves. One day Tony looked across the library and saw Dewey on top of the wall shelves at the opposite end of the building. That was when things changed for Dewey, when he realized he could climb to the top of the wall shelves whenever he wanted. He had the run of the library up there, and some days he never wanted to come down.

'Where's Dewey?' each member of the genealogy club would ask as they settled in for their regular meeting on the first Saturday of the month. Like all the clubs that met in the library – our Round Room was the largest free meeting space in town, and it was usually booked – the club members were used to the Dewey treatment. This started with Dewey jumping into the center of the table at the beginning of every meeting. He would survey the meeting participants, then walk around to each person at the table, sniffing her hand or looking into his face. When he had made a full circuit, he chose one person and settled into his lap. It didn't matter what was going on in the meeting, Dewey never rushed or varied his routine. The only way to break his rhythm was to toss him out and close the door.

The Dewey treatment was met with resistance at first, especially by the business and political groups that often met in the Round Room, but after a few months even the salesmen treated it as a highlight. The genealogy club treated it almost like a game, since every month Dewey picked someone different to spend the meeting with. They would laugh and try to coax him into their laps, almost like the children at Story Hour.

'Dewey's distracted these days,' I told them. 'Ever since Tony started painting the library, he's been off his routine. But I'm sure once he realizes you're here . . .'

And as if on cue, Dewey walked in the door, jumped on the table, and started his rounds.

'Let us know if you need anything,' I told them, turning back to the main part of the library. Nobody said anything; they were too busy focusing on Dewey. 'No fair, Esther,' I heard as the sound of the meeting faded into the distance, 'you must have tuna in your pocket.'

When Tony finished the painting three weeks later, Dewey was a changed cat. Maybe he thought he really was a Duke, because suddenly he wasn't content with just naps and laps. He wanted to explore. And climb. And most important, explore new places to climb. We called this Dewey's Edmund Hillary phase, after the famous mountain climber. Dewey didn't want to stop climbing until he'd reached the top of his personal Mount Everest, which he managed to do not more than a month later.

'Any sign of Dewey this morning?' I asked Audrey Wheeler, who was working at the circulation desk. 'He didn't come for breakfast.'

'I haven't seen him.'

'Let me know if you do. I want to make sure he's not sick.'

Five minutes later I heard Audrey utter what around here was a surprising profanity: 'Oh, my goodness!'

She was standing in the middle of the library, looking straight up. And there, on top of the lights, looking straight down, was Dewey.

When he saw us looking, Dewey pulled his head back. He was instantly invisible. As we watched, Dewey's head reappeared a few feet down the light. Then it disappeared again, only to appear a few feet farther on. The lights run in hundred-foot strips, and he had clearly been up there for hours, watching us.

'How are we going to get him down?'

'Maybe we should call the city,' someone suggested. 'They'll send someone with a ladder.'

'Let's just wait him out,' I said. 'He's not doing any harm up there, and he'll have to come down for food eventually.'

An hour later Dewey trotted into my office, licking his lips from a late breakfast, and jumped into my lap for a pet. He was clearly keyed up about this new game, but didn't want to overplay his hand. I knew he was dying to ask, *What do you think of that?*

'I'm not even going to mention it, Dewey.'

He cocked his head at me.

'I'm serious.'

Okay then, I'll nap. Exciting morning, you know.

I asked around, but nobody had seen him come down. It took us a few weeks of constant surveillance to figure out his method of getting up. First Dewey jumped on the empty computer desk. Then he jumped on a filing cabinet, which gave him a long jump to the top of the temporary wall around the staff area, where he could hide behind a huge quilt of Spencer history. From there, it was only four feet to the light.

Sure, we could have rearranged the furniture, but once he became ceiling fixated we knew there wasn't much, except old age and creaky bones, that could stop Dewey from walking the lights. When cats don't know something exists, it's easy to keep them away. If they can't get to something and it's something they've made up their minds they want, it's almost impossible. Cats aren't lazy; they'll put in the work to thwart even the best-laid plans.

Besides, Dewey loved being up on the lights. He loved walking back and forth from end to end until he found an interesting spot. Then he would lie down, drape his head over the side, and watch. The patrons loved it, too. Sometimes when Dewey was pacing you could see them craning up at the ceiling, their heads going back and forth like the pendulum on a clock. They talked to him. When Dewey was pointed out to the children, his head just peaking over the edge of the lights, they screamed with excitement. They had so many questions.

'What's he doing?'

'How'd he get up there?'

'Why is he up there?'

'Will he get burned?'

'What if he falls off? Will he die?'

'What if he falls on somebody? Will they die?'

When the children found out they couldn't join him on the ceiling, they begged him to come down. 'Dewey likes it up there,' we explained. 'He's playing.' Eventually even the children understood that when Dewey was on the lights, he was coming down only on his terms. He had discovered his own little seventh heaven up there.

The official remodeling took place in July 1989, because July was the library's slow month. The children were out of school, which meant no class trips and no unofficial after-school child care. A local tax firm donated warehouse space across the street. The Spencer Public Library contained 55 shelving units, 50,000 books, 6,000 magazines, 2,000 newspapers, 5,000 albums and cassette tapes, and 1,000 genealogy books and binders, not to mention projectors, movie screens, televisions, cameras (16 mm and 8 mm), typewriters, desks, tables, chairs, card catalogs, filing cabinets, and office supplies. Everything was given a number. The number corresponded to a color-coordinated grid, which showed both its place in the warehouse and its new place in the library. On the new blue carpet, Jean Hollis Clark and I chalked the location of every shelf, table, and desk. If a shelf was put down an inch out of place, the workers had to move it because there were strict aisle width and ADA (Americans with Disabilities Act) requirements. If a shelf was off an inch, the next one could be off two inches. Next thing you knew, a wheelchair would be stuck in a back corner.

The move was truly a community effort. The Rotary Club helped move the books out; the Golden Kiwanis helped move them back. Our downtown development manager, Bob Rose, moved shelving. Doris Armstrong's husband, Jerry, spent more than a week bolting 110 new steel plates onto the ends of our shelving units, at least six bolts per plate, and never complained. Everybody volunteered: the genealogy club, the library board, teachers, parents, the nine-member board of Spencer's Friends of the Library. The downtown merchants pitched in, too, and there were free drinks and snacks for everyone.

The remodeling went like clockwork. In exactly three weeks, our Halloween horror was replaced with a neutral blue carpet and colorful reupholstered furniture. We added two-person gliders to the children's library so mothers could rock and read to their kids. In a closet, I found eighteen Grosvenor prints, along with seven old pen-and-ink sketches. The library didn't have enough money to frame them, so each print was adopted by a member of the community who paid for the framing. The newly arranged, angled shelves led the eye back into the books, where thousands of colorful spines invited patrons to browse, read, relax.

We unveiled the new library with a cookies and tea open house. Nobody was more excited that day than Dewey. He had been locked away at my house for three weeks, and during that time his whole world had changed. The walls were different; the carpet was different; all the chairs and tables and bookshelves were out of place. The books even smelled different after a trip to the warehouse across the street.

But as soon as people started arriving, Dewey dashed back to the refreshment table to be front and center again. Yes, the library had changed, but what he missed most after three weeks away was people. He hated being away from his friends at the library. And they had missed him, too. As they went for their cookies, they all stopped to pet Dewey. Some lifted him onto their shoulders for a tour through the newly arranged shelving units. Others just watched him, talked about him, and smiled. The library may have changed, but Dewey was still the king.

Between 1987, the year before Dewey fell into our arms, and 1989, the year of the remodel, visits to the Spencer Public Library increased from 63,000 a year to more than 100,000. Clearly something had changed. People were thinking differently about their library, appreciating it more. And not just the citizens of Spencer. That year, 19.4 percent of our visitors were from rural Clay County. Another 18 percent came from the surrounding counties. No one could argue, seeing those numbers, that the library wasn't a regional center.

The remodeling helped, there's no doubt about that. So did the revitalization of Grand Avenue; and the economy, which was picking up; and the energized staff; and our new outreach and entertainment programs. But most of the change, most of what brought the new people in and finally made the Spencer Public Library a meeting house, not a warehouse, was Dewey.

14

Dewey's Great Escape

Late July is the best time of year in Spencer. The corn is ten feet high, golden and green. It's so high, the farmers are required by state law to cut it to half height every mile, where the roads meet at right angles. Rural Iowa has too many intersections and not enough stop signs. The short corn helps, because at least you can see cars coming, and it doesn't hurt the farmers. Corn ears grow in the center of the stalk, not the top.

It's easy to neglect your job in an Iowa summer. The bright green, the warm sun, the endless fields. You leave the windows open, just to catch the scent.

You spend your lunch hour down by the river, your weekends fishing near Thunder Bridge. It's hard, sometimes, to stay inside.

'Is this heaven?' I want to say every year.

'No,' is the imaginary reply. 'It's Iowa.'

By August of 1989, the remodeling effort was over. Attendance was up. The staff was happy. Dewey had not only been accepted by the community, but was drawing people in and inspiring them. The Clay County Fair, the biggest event of the year, was just around the corner in September. I even had a month off from my master's classes. Everything was going perfectly – except for Dewey. My contented baby boy, our library hero, was a changed cat: distracted, jumpy, and most of all, trouble.

The problem was the three weeks Dewey had spent at my house during the remodeling, staring through my window screens at the world outside. He couldn't see the corn from my house, but he could hear the birds. He could feel the breeze. He could smell whatever cats smell when they direct their nose to the great outdoors. Now he missed those screens. There were windows in the library, but they didn't open. You could smell the new carpet but not the outdoors. You could hear trucks, but you couldn't make out the birds. *How can you show me something so wonderful,* he seemed to whine, *then take it away?*

Between the two sets of front doors at the Spencer Public Library was a tiny glass lobby that helped keep out the cold in the winter, since at least one set of doors was usually closed. For two years Dewey hated that lobby; when he returned from his three weeks at my house, he adored it. From the lobby, he could hear the birds. When the outer doors were open, he could smell fresh air. For a few hours in the afternoon, there was even a patch of sunlight. He pretended that was all he wanted, to sit in that patch of sunlight and listen to the birds. But we knew better. If he spent enough time in the lobby, Dewey would become curious about going through that second set of doors and into the outside world.

'Dewey, get back in here!' the front desk clerk would yell every time he followed a patron out the first set of doors. The poor cat had no chance. The circulation desk faced into the lobby, and the desk clerk always spotted him immediately. So Dewey stopped listening, especially if the clerk was Joy DeWall. Joy was the newest and youngest member of the staff and the only one who wasn't married. She lived with her parents in a duplex where the lease didn't allow pets, so she had a soft spot in her heart for Dewey. Dewey knew that, and he wouldn't listen to a word she said. So Joy started coming back to get me. I was the Mom voice. Dewey always listened to me, although in this case he was so intent on disobeying I was forced to back up my threat.

'Dewey, do you want me to get the squirt bottle?'

He just stared at me.

I brought the squirt bottle out from behind my back. With the other arm, I held open the door to the library. Dewey slunk back inside.

Ten minutes later I heard: 'Vicki, Dewey's in the lobby again.'

That was it. Three times in one day. It was time to put my foot down. I stormed out of my office, screwed up my best Mom voice, threw open the lobby door, and demanded, 'You get in here right now, young man.'

A man in his early twenties almost jumped out of his skin. Before the last word was out of my mouth, he had rushed into the library, grabbed a magazine, and buried his head in it all the way up to the fine print. Talk about embarrassing. I was holding the door open in stunned silence, unable to believe I hadn't seen this kid right in front of my face, when Dewey came trotting past like nothing out of the ordinary had happened. I could almost see him smiling.

A week later, Dewey didn't come for his morning meal, and I couldn't find him anywhere. Nothing unusual there; Dewey had plenty of places to hide. There was a cubbyhole behind the display case by the front door that I swear was the size of a box of crayons – the old sixty-four pack with the sharpener built in. There was the brown lounge chair in the children's area, although his tail usually stuck out of that one. One afternoon Joy was shelving the bottom row of books in the Westerns section when, to her amazement, Dewey popped out. In a library, books fit on both sides of a shelf. Between the two rows is four inches of space. Between the books was Dewey's ultimate hiding place: quick, handy, and secure. The only way to find him was to lift books at random and look behind them. That doesn't sound so difficult until you consider that the Spencer Public Library contained more than four hundred shelves of books. Between those books was an enormous labyrinth, a long, narrow world all Dewey's own.

Fortunately he almost always stuck to his favorite place in the bottom rows of Westerns. Not this time. He wasn't under the brown lounger, either, or in his cubbyhole. I didn't notice him peeking down from the lights. I opened the doors to the bathrooms to see if he had been locked inside. Not this morning.

'Has anyone seen Dewey?'

No. No. No. No.

'Who locked up last night?'

'I did,' Joy said, 'and he was definitely here.' I knew Joy would never have forgotten to look for Dewey. She was the only staffer, besides me, who would stay late with him to play hide-and-seek.

'Good. He must be in the building. Looks like he's found a new hiding place.'

But when I returned from lunch, Dewey was still missing. And he hadn't touched his food. That's when I began to worry.

'Where's Dewey?' a patron asked.

We had already heard that question twenty times, and it was only early afternoon. I told the staff, 'Tell them Dewey's not feeling well. No need to alarm anyone.' He'd show up. I knew it.

That night, I drove around for half an hour instead of heading straight home. I wasn't expecting to see a fluffy orange cat prowling the neighborhood, but you never know. The thought going through my mind was, 'What if he's hurt? What if he needs me, and I can't find him? I'm letting him down.' I knew he wasn't dead. He was so healthy. And I knew he hadn't run away. But the thought kept creeping up. . . .

He wasn't waiting for me at the front door the next day. I stepped inside and the place felt dead. A cold dread walked up my spine, even though it was ninety degrees outside. I knew something was wrong.

I told the staff, 'Look everywhere.'

We checked every corner. We opened every cabinet and drawer. We pulled books off the shelves, hoping to find him in his crawl space. We shone a flashlight behind the wall shelves. Some of them had pulled an inch or two away from the wall; Dewey could have been making his rounds, fallen in, and gotten stuck. Clumsiness wasn't like him, but in an emergency you check every possibility.

The night janitor! The thought hit me like a rock, and I picked up the phone. 'Hi, Virgil, it's Vicki at the library. Did you see Dewey last night?'

'Who?'

'Dewey. The cat.'

'Nope. Didn't see him.'

'Is there anything he could have gotten into that made him sick? Cleaning solution maybe?'

He hesitated. 'Don't think so.'

I didn't want to ask, but I had to. 'Do you ever leave any doors open?'

He really hesitated this time. 'I prop open the back door when I take the garbage to the Dumpster.'

'How long?'

'Maybe five minutes.'

'Did you prop it open two nights ago?'

'I prop it every night.'

My heart sank. That was it. Dewey would never just run out an open door, but if he had a few weeks to think about it, peek around the corner, sniff the air . . .

'Do you think he ran out?' Virgil asked.

'Yes, Virgil, I do.'

I told the staff the news. Any information was good for our spirits. We set up shifts so that two people could cover the library while the rest looked for Dewey. The regular patrons could tell something was wrong. 'Where's Dewey?' went from an innocent inquiry to an expression of concern. We continued to tell most patrons nothing was wrong, but we took the regulars aside and told them Dewey was missing. Soon a dozen people were walking the sidewalks. 'Look at all these people. Look at all this love. We'll find him now,' I told myself again and again.

I was wrong.

I spent my lunch hour walking the streets, looking for my baby boy. He was so sheltered in the library. He wasn't a fighter. He was a finicky eater. How was he going to survive?

On the kindness of strangers, of course. Dewey trusted people. He wouldn't hesitate to ask for help.

I dropped in on Mr. Fonley at Fonley Flowers, which had a back entrance off the alley behind the library. He hadn't seen Dewey. Neither had Rick Krebsbach at the photo studio. I called all the veterinarians in town. We didn't have an animal shelter, so a vet's office was the place someone would take him. If they didn't recognize him, that is. I told the vets, 'If someone brings in a cat who looks like Dewey, it probably is Dewey. We think he's escaped.'

I told myself, 'Everyone knows Dewey. Everyone loves Dewey. If someone finds him, they'll bring him back to the library.'

I didn't want to spread the news that he was missing. Dewey had so many children who loved him, not to mention the special needs students. Oh, my goodness, what about Crystal? I didn't want to scare them. I knew Dewey was coming back.

When Dewey wasn't waiting for me at the front door on the third morning, my stomach plummeted. I realized that, in my heart, I had been expecting to see him sitting there. When he wasn't, I was devastated. That's when it hit me: Dewey was gone. He might be dead. He probably wasn't coming back. I knew Dewey was important, but only at that moment did I realize how big a hole he would leave. To the town of Spencer, Dewey was the library. How could we go on without him?

When Jodi was three, I lost her at the Mankato Mall. I looked down and she was gone. I almost choked on my own heart, it jumped into my throat so fast. When I couldn't find her, I became absolutely frantic. My baby. My baby. I couldn't even think. All I could do was rip clothes off hangers, run the aisles faster and faster. I finally found her hiding in the middle of a circular rack of clothes, laughing. She had been there all along. But, oh, how I died when I thought she was gone.

I felt the same way now. That's when I realized Dewey wasn't just the library's cat. My grief wasn't for the town of Spencer, or for its library, or even for its children. The grief was for me. He might live at the library, but Dewey was my cat. I loved him. That's not just words. I didn't just love something about him. I loved him. But my baby boy, my baby Dewey, was gone.

The mood in the library was black. Yesterday we had hope. We believed it was only a matter of time. Now we believed he was gone. We continued to search, but we had looked everywhere. We were out of options. I sat down and thought about what I was going to tell the community. I would call the radio station, which was the information nexus of Spencer. They would immediately make an announcement. They could mention an orange cat without saying his name. The adults would understand, but maybe that would buy time with the children.

'Vicki!'

Then the newspaper. They would definitely run the story tomorrow. Maybe someone had taken him in.

'Vicki!'

Should we put up flyers? What about a reward?

'Vicki!'

Who was I kidding? He was gone. If he was here, we would have found . . .

'Vicki! Guess who's home!'

I stuck my head out of the office and there he was, my big orange buddy, wrapped in the arms of Jean Hollis Clark. I rushed over and hugged him tight. He laid his head on my chest. Out of the circular clothes rack, right under my nose, my child had appeared!

'Oh, baby boy, baby boy. Don't ever do that again.'

Dewey didn't need me to reassure him. I could tell immediately this was no joke. Dewey was purring like he had on our first morning. He was so happy to see me, so thankful to be in my arms. He seemed happy. But I knew him so well. Underneath, in his bones, he was still shaking.

'I found him under a car on Grand Avenue,' Jean was saying. 'I was going over to White Drug, and I happened to catch a glimpse of orange out of the corner of my eye.'

I wasn't listening. I would hear the story many times over the next few days, but at that moment I wasn't listening. I only had eyes and ears for Dewey.

'He was hunched against the wheel on the far side of the car. I called to him, but he didn't come. He looked like he wanted to run, but he was too afraid. He must have been right there all along. Can you believe that? All those people looking for him, and he was right there all along.'

The rest of the staff was crowding around us now. I could tell they wanted to hold him, to cuddle him, but I didn't want to let him go.

'He needs to eat,' I told them. Someone put out a fresh can of food, and we all watched while Dewey sucked it down. I doubt the cat had eaten in days.

Once he had done his business – food, water, litter box – I let the staff hold him. He was passed from hand to hand like a hero in a victory parade. When everyone had welcomed him home, we took him out to show the public. Most of them didn't know anything had happened, but there were a few wet eyes. Dewey, our prodigal son, gone but now returned to us. You really do love something more when it's been lost.

That afternoon I gave Dewey a bath, which he tolerated for the first time since that cold January morning so long ago. He was covered in motor oil, which took months to work out of his long fur. He had a tear in one ear and a scratch on his nose. I cleaned them gently and lovingly. Was it another cat? A loose wire? The undercarriage of a car? I rubbed his cut ear between my fingers, and Dewey didn't even flinch. 'What happened out there?' I wanted to ask him, but the two of us had already come to an understanding. We would never talk about this incident again.

Years later, I would make it a habit to prop open a side door during library board meetings. Cathy Greiner, a board member, asked me every time, 'Aren't you worried Dewey will run out?'

I looked down at Dewey, who was there as usual to attend the meeting, and he looked up at me. That look told me, as clearly as if he'd crossed his heart and hoped to die, that he wasn't going to run. Why couldn't everyone else see it?

'He's not going anywhere,' I told her. 'He's committed to the library.'

And he was. For sixteen years, Dewey never went into the lobby again. He lounged by the front door, especially in the morning, but he never followed patrons out. If the doors opened and he heard trucks, he sprinted to the staff area. He didn't want to be anywhere near a passing truck. Dewey was completely done with the outdoors.

15

Spencer's Favorite Cat

About a month after Dewey's escape, Jodi left Spencer. I wasn't sure I could afford to send her to college, and she didn't want to stay home. Jodi wanted to travel, so she took a job as a nanny in California and saved money for college. I'm sure it didn't hurt that California was a long way from Mom.

I brought Dewey home for her last weekend. As always, he was stuck to Jodi's side like a flesh-hugging magnet. I think he loved nighttime with her most of all. As soon as Jodi pulled down the covers, Dewey was in her bed. Actually he beat her into bed. By the time she finished brushing her teeth, he was sitting on her pillow, ready to curl up beside her. As soon as she lay down, he was plastered against her face. He wouldn't even let her breathe. She shoved him down into the covers, but he came back. Shove. On her face. Shove. Across her neck.

'Stay down, Dewey.'

He finally relented and slept by her side, locked onto her hip. She could breathe, but she couldn't turn over. Did he know our girl was leaving, maybe for good? When he slept with me, Dewey was in and out of bed all night, exploring the house one minute and snuggling the next. With Jodi, he never left. At one point, he wandered down to attack her feet, which were under the covers, but that was as far as he went. Jodi didn't get any sleep that night.

The next time Dewey came to my house, Jodi was gone. He found a way to stay close to her, though, by spending the night in Jodi's room, curled up on the floor next to her heater, no doubt dreaming of those warm summer nights spent snuggled up to Jodi's side.

'I know, Dewey,' I said to him. 'I know.'

A month later I took Dewey for his first official photograph. I'd like to say it was for sentimental reasons, that my world was changing and I wanted to freeze that moment, or that I realized Dewey was on the cusp of something far bigger than either of us ever imagined. But the real reason was a coupon. Rick Krebsbach, the town photographer, was offering pet photographs for ten dollars.

Dewey was such an easygoing cat that I convinced myself getting a professional portrait made of him, in a professional portrait studio, would be easy. But Dewey hated the studio. As soon as we walked in, his head was swiveling, his eyes looking at everything. I put him in the chair, and he immediately hopped out. I picked him up and put him in the chair again. I took one step back, and Dewey was gone.

'He's nervous. He hasn't been out of the library much,' I said as I watched Dewey sniff the photo backdrop.

'That's nothing,' Rick said.

'Pets aren't easy?'

'You have no idea,' he said as we watched Dewey dig his head under a pillow. 'One dog tried to eat my camera. Another dog actually ate my fake flowers. Now that I think about it, he puked on that pillow.'

I picked Dewey up quickly, but my touch didn't calm him. He was still looking around, more nervous than interested.

'There's been quite a bit of unfortunate peeing. I had to throw away a sheet. I sanitize everything, of course, but to an animal like Dewey it must smell like a zoo.'

'He's not used to other animals,' I said, but I knew that wasn't quite right. Dewey never cared about other animals. He always ignored the Seeing Eye dog who came into the library. He even ignored the Dalmatian. This wasn't fear; it was confusion. 'He knows what's expected of him in the library, but he doesn't understand this place.'

'Take your time.'

A thought. 'May I show Dewey the camera?'

'If you think it will help.'

Dewey posed for photographs at the library all the time, but those were personal cameras. Rick's camera was a large, boxy, professional model. Dewey had never seen one of those before, but he was a fast learner.

'It's a camera, Dewey. Camera. We're here to get your picture taken.'

Dewey sniffed the lens. He leaned back and looked at it, then sniffed it again. I could feel him getting less tense, and I knew he understood.

I pointed. 'Chair. Sit in the chair.'

I put him down. He sniffed up and down every leg, and twice on the seat. Then he jumped into the chair and stared right at the camera. Rick hurried over and snapped six photos.

'I can't believe it,' he said as Dewey climbed down off the chair.

I didn't want to tell Rick, but this happened all the time. Dewey and I had a means of communicating even I didn't understand. He always seemed to know what I wanted, but unfortunately that didn't mean he was always going to obey. I didn't even have to say *brush* or *bath*; all I had to do was think about them, and Dewey disappeared. I remember passing him in the library one afternoon. He looked up at me with his usual lazy indifference. *Hi, how you doing?*

I thought, 'Oh, there are two knots of fur on his neck. I should get the scissors and cut them off.' As soon as the idea formed in my mind, *whoosh*, Dewey was gone.

But since his escape, Dewey had been using his powers for good, not mischief. He not only anticipated what I wanted, he did it. Not when a brushing or a bath was involved, of course, but for library business. That was one reason he was so willing to have his photograph taken. He wanted to do what was best for the library.

'He knows it's for the library,' I told Rick, but I could tell he wasn't buying it. Why, after all, would a cat care about a library? And how could he connect a library with a photo studio a block away? But it was the truth, and I knew it.

I picked Dewey up and petted his favorite spot, the top of his head between the ears. 'He knows what a camera is. He's not afraid of it.'

'Has he ever posed before?'

'At least two or three times a week. For visitors. He loves it.'

'That doesn't sound like a cat.'

I wanted to tell him Dewey wasn't just any cat, but Rick had been taking pet photographs for the past week. He'd probably heard it a hundred times already.

And yet if you see Dewey's official photograph, which Rick shot that day (it's on the cover of this book), you can tell immediately he's not just another cat. He's beautiful, yes, but more than that, he's relaxed. He has no fear of the camera, no confusion about what's going on. His eyes are wide and clear. His fur is perfectly groomed. He doesn't look like a kitten, but he doesn't look like a grown cat, either. He's a young man getting his college graduation photograph taken, or a sailor getting a memento for his girl back home before shipping off on his first tour. His posture is remarkably straight, his head cocked, his eyes staring calmly into the camera. I smile every time I see that photo because he looks so serious. He looks like he's trying to be strong and handsome but can't quite pull it off because he's so darn cute.

A few days after receiving the finished photographs, I noticed the local Shopko, a large general merchandise chain like Wal-Mart or Kmart, was holding a pet photo contest to raise money for charity. You paid a dollar to vote, and the money was used to fight muscular dystrophy. This was typical of Spencer. There was always a fund-raiser, and it was always supported by local citizens. Our radio station, KCID, promoted these efforts. The paper often ran a story. The turnout was usually overwhelming. We don't have a ton of money in Spencer, but if someone needs a hand, we're happy to provide it. That's civic pride.

On a whim, I entered Dewey in the contest. The photo was for library promotion purposes, after all, and wasn't this a perfect opportunity to promote this special aspect of the library? A few weeks later, Shopko strung a dozen photos, all of cats and dogs,

on a wire in the front of the store. The town voted,
and Dewey won by a landslide. He got more than
80 percent of the votes, seven times as many as the
runner-up. It was ridiculous. When the store called to
tell me the results, I was almost embarrassed.

Part of the reason Dewey won so overwhelmingly
was the photograph. Dewey is staring at you, asking
you to look back at him. He makes a personal
connection, even if there is a touch of stateliness in
his pose.

Part of the reason was Dewey's looks. He's a 1950s
matinee idol, suave and cool. He's so handsome you
have to love him.

Part of the reason was Dewey's personality. Most
cats in photographs look scared to death, desperate to
sniff the camera, or disgusted by the whole process –
or often all three. Most dogs look like they are about
to go absolutely bonkers, knock over everything in
the room, get themselves wound up in an electrical
cord, and then eat the camera. Dewey looks calm.

But mostly, Dewey trounced the competition
because the town had adopted him. Not just the
regular library patrons, I realized for the first time,
but the whole town. While I wasn't watching, while
I was preoccupied with school and remodeling and
Jodi, Dewey was quietly working his magic. The
stories, not just about his rescue but about his life
and relationships, were seeping down into the cracks
and sprouting new life. He wasn't just the library's
cat, not anymore. He was Spencer's cat. He was our

inspiration, our friend, our survivor. He was one of us. And at the same time, he was ours.

Was he a mascot? No. Did he make a difference in the way the town thought about itself? Absolutely. Not to everyone, of course, but to enough. Dewey reminded us, once again, that we were a different kind of town. We cared. We valued the small things. We understood life wasn't about quantity but quality. Dewey was one more reason to love this hardy little town on the Iowa plains. The love of Spencer, the love of Dewey, it was all intermingled in the public mind.

16

Iowa's Famous Library Cat

I can see now, in hindsight, that Dewey's escape was a turning point, a last fling at the end of youth. After that, he was content with his lot in life: to be the cat in residence at the Spencer Public Library, a friend, a confidant, and a goodwill ambassador to all. He greeted people with new enthusiasm. He perfected the fine art of lounging in the middle of adult nonfiction, where he could be seen from the whole library, but where there was plenty of room for people to walk without stepping on him. If he was in a contemplative mood, he would lie on his stomach with his head up and his front paws crossed casually in front. We called this his Buddha pose. Dewey could zone out in that pose for an hour like a fat little man at peace with the world. His other favorite position was to sprawl out full on his back, wide open, his paws sticking out in four directions. He went completely slack, letting it all hang out.

It's amazing how, when you stop running and start sprawling, the world comes to you. Or if not the world, then at least Iowa. Soon after the Shopko contest, Dewey was the subject of Chuck Offenburger's Iowa Boy column in the *Des Moines Register.* Iowa Boy was one of those columns that said things like, 'It was the most shocking piece of news I'd come across since the time a few years ago I found out the Cleghorn Public Library, just down the road a ways, had started checking out cake pans to its patrons.' In fact, that's exactly what the column said, and yes, the Cleghorn Public Library, just down the road, does check out cake pans to patrons. I know at least a dozen libraries in Iowa with extensive cake pan collections. The librarians hang them on the walls. If you want to bake a special cake, for instance, a Winnie the Pooh cake for a child's birthday party, you go to the library. Now, those are librarians who serve their communities!

When I read the article, I thought, 'Wow, Dewey's really made it.' It was one thing for a town to adopt a cat. It was even better for a region to adopt that cat, as northwest Iowa had with Dewey. The library received visitors every day from small towns and farms in surrounding counties. Summer residents of the Iowa lake country drove down to meet him, then spread the word to their neighbors and guests, who would drive down the following week. He appeared frequently in the newspapers of nearby towns. But the *Des Moines Register*! That was the daily newspaper in the state capital, which had a population of almost 500,000. The *Des Moines Register* was read all over the state. More than half a million people were probably reading about Dewey right now. That was more people than attend the Clay County Fair!

After Iowa Boy, Dewey started making regular appearances on our local television newscasts, which originated out of Sioux City, Iowa, and Sioux Falls, South Dakota. Soon he began appearing on stations in other nearby cities and states. Every segment started the same way, with a voice-over: *The Spencer Library wasn't expecting anything more in their drop box than books on a freezing January morning* . . . . No matter how they framed it, the picture was the same. A poor feeble kitten, almost frozen to death, begging for help. The story of Dewey's arrival at the library was irresistible.

But so was his personality. Most news crews weren't used to filming cats – there were thousands of cats in northwest Iowa, no doubt, but none ever made it on camera – so they always started out with what seemed like a good idea: 'Just have him act natural.'

'Well, there he is, sleeping in a box with his tail hanging out and his stomach oozing over the side. That's as natural as it gets.'

Five seconds later: 'Maybe he can jump or something?'

Dewey always gave them what they wanted. He jumped over the camera for a flying action shot. He walked between two displays to show his dexterity. He ran and jumped off the end of a shelf. He played with a child. He played with his red yarn. He sat quietly on top of the computer and stared into the camera, the model of decorum. He wasn't showing off. Posing for the camera was part of Dewey's job as publicity director for the library, so he did it. Enthusiastically.

Dewey's appearance on *Living in Iowa*, an Iowa Public Television series that focuses on issues, events, and people in the state of Iowa, was typical. The *Living in Iowa* crew met me at the library at seven thirty in the morning. Dewey was ready. He rolled. He jumped between the shelves. He walked up and put his nose on the camera. He stuck right by the side of the host, a beautiful young woman, winning her over.

'Can I hold him?' she asked.

I showed her the Dewey Carry – over the left shoulder, with his behind in the crook of your arm, head over your back. If you wanted to hold him for any length of time, you had to use the Dewey Carry.

'He's doing it!' the host whispered excitedly as Dewey draped over her shoulder.

Dewey's head popped up. *What did she say?*

'How do I get him to calm down?'

'Just pet him.'

The host stroked his back. Dewey lay his head on her shoulder and cuddled against her neck. 'He's doing it! He's really doing it! I can feel him purring.' She smiled at her cameraman and whispered, 'Are you getting this?'

I was tempted to tell her, 'Of course he's doing it. He does it for everyone,' but why spoil her excitement?

Dewey's episode aired a few months later. It was called 'A Tale of Two Kitties.' (Yes, it's a pun on Charles Dickens.) The other kitty was Tom, who lived in Kibby's Hardware in Conrad, Iowa, a small town in the middle of the state. Like Dewey, Tom was found on the coldest night of the year. Store owner Ralph Kibby took the frozen stray to the vet's office. 'They gave him sixty dollars' worth of shots,' he said on the program, 'and said if he's still alive in the morning he may have a chance.' As I watched the show, I realized why the host was so happy that morning. There were at least thirty seconds of footage of Dewey lying on her shoulder; the best she could get from Tom was a sniff of her finger.

Dewey wasn't the only one expanding his horizons. During my master's program I had become very active in state library circles, and after graduation I was elected president of the Iowa Small Library Association, an advocacy group for libraries in towns of less than 10,000 people. Advocacy, at least when I joined, was a stretch. The group had a serious inferiority complex. 'We're small,' they thought. 'Who cares about us? Let's just stick with milk, cookies, and a little gossip. That's all we're good for.'

But I had seen firsthand that small didn't mean irrelevant, and I was inspired. 'You don't think small towns matter?' I asked them. 'You don't think your library can make a difference? Look at Dewey. Every librarian in the state knows Dewey Readmore Books. He's appeared on the cover of the Iowa library newsletter twice. He appeared twice in the National Library Cat Society newsletter, and he gets fan mail from England and Belgium. He was featured in the state library newsletter . . . of Illinois. I get calls every week from librarians wondering how they can convince their board to let them have a cat. Does that sound irrelevant to you?'

'So we should all get cats?'

'No. You should believe in yourselves.'

And they did. Two years later, the Iowa Small Library Association was one of the most active and respected advocacy groups in the state.

Dewey's breakthrough, though, came not through my efforts but through the mail. One afternoon the library received a package containing twenty copies of the June/July 1990 issue of *Country*, a national magazine with a circulation of more than five million. It wasn't unusual for us to receive magazines from publishers hoping to drum up library subscriptions, but twenty copies? I had never read *Country*, and I had never spoken to anyone from *Country*, but I liked its slogan: For Those Who Live In or Long For The Country. I decided to flip through it. Right there, on page 57, was a two-page, full-color article about Dewey Readmore Books of the Spencer Public Library, complete with photographs sent in by a local woman I didn't even know but whose daughter frequented the library. Clearly she had been going home and telling her mother about the Dew.

It was just a small article, but its impact was extraordinary. For years, visitors told me how much it inspired them. Writers, calling for information for other articles about Dewey, often cited it. More than a decade later, I opened the mail to find a perfectly preserved copy of the article, neatly torn out of the magazine near the fold. The woman wanted me to know how much Dewey's story meant to her.

In Spencer, people who had forgotten about Dewey or who had never shown any interest in him took notice. Even the crowd at Sister's Café perked up. The worst of the farm crisis had passed, and our leaders were looking for a way to attract new business. Dewey was getting the kind of national exposure they could only dream of, and of course that energy and excitement was rubbing off on the town. Sure, nobody has ever built a factory because of a cat, but nobody has ever built a factory in a town they'd never heard of, either. Once again, Dewey was doing his part, not just in Spencer this time but out there in the larger world, beyond the cornfields of Iowa.

The biggest change, though, was pride. Dewey's friends were proud of him, and everyone was proud to have him in town. One man, back for his twentieth high school reunion, stopped by the library to flip through newspapers from that year. Dewey, of course, won him over immediately. But once he heard about Dewey's friends and saw the articles about him, he became truly impressed. He wrote later to thank us and say he'd been telling everyone in New York about his wonderful hometown and its beloved library cat.

He wasn't the only one. We had three or four people a week coming into the library to show Dewey off. 'We're here to see the famous cat,' an older man said, approaching the desk.

'He's sleeping in the back. I'll go get him.'

'Thanks,' he said, motioning to a younger woman with a little blond girl hiding behind her leg. 'I wanted my granddaughter Lydia to meet him. She's in town from Kentucky.'

When Lydia saw Dewey, she smiled and looked up at her grandfather as if for permission. 'Go ahead, sweetie. Dewey won't bite.' The girl tentatively stretched out her hand to Dewey; two minutes later she was stretched out on the floor, petting him.

'See?' her grandfather said to the little girl's mother. 'I told you it was worth the trip.' I suppose he could have meant Dewey or the library, but I suspect he was referring to something more.

Later, while the mother was petting Dewey with her daughter, the grandfather came up to me and said, 'Thanks so much for adopting Dewey.' It seemed he wanted to say more, but I think we both understood he had already said enough. Thirty minutes later, as they were leaving, I heard the young woman tell the older man, 'You were right, Dad. That was great. I wish we had come by sooner.'

'Don't worry, Mommy,' the little girl said. 'We'll see him next year, too.'

Pride. Confidence. Assurance that this cat, this library, this experience, maybe even this town, really was special. Dewey wasn't any more beautiful or friendly after the *Country* article; in fact, fame never changed him. All Dewey ever wanted was a warm place to nap, a fresh can of food, and love and attention from every person who ever stepped foot in the Spencer Public Library. But at the same time, Dewey *had* changed, because now people looked at him differently.

The proof? Before the *Country* article, nobody took the blame for shoving poor Dewey into our book return. Everybody knew the story, but nobody confessed. After Dewey hit the media, eleven different people came up to me confidentially and swore on their mother's grave (or their mother's eye, if Mom was alive) that they had shoved Dewey down that hole. They weren't taking blame; they were taking credit. 'I always knew it would turn out well,' they said.

Eleven people! Can you believe it? That must have been one wild, cat-saving alley party.

THE DAILY ROUTINE

As developed by Dewey Readmore Books
soon after his regrettable romp outside
the Spencer Public Library, and
followed for the rest of his life.

7:30 a.m. Mom Arrives. Demand food, but
don't be too hasty. Watch everything she
does. Follow at her heels. Make her feel
special.

8:00 a.m. Staff Arrives. Spend an hour
checking in with everyone. Find out who
is having a tough morning and give them
the honor of petting me for as long as they
want. Or until . . .

8:58 a.m. Prep Time. Take up position by
the front door, ready for first patron of the
day. Also has the added benefit of alerting
distracted staff to current time. I hate it
when they open late.

9:00–10:30 a.m. Doors Open. Greet patrons.
Follow the nice ones, ignore the mean ones,
but give everyone a chance to brighten their
day by paying attention to me. Petting me is
a gift to you for visiting the library.

10:30 a.m. Find Lap for Nap. Laps are for naps, not playing. Playing in laps is for kittens.

11:30–11:45 a.m. Lounge. Middle of adult nonfiction, head up, paws crossed in front. The humans call this the Buddha pose. I call it the Lion. Hakuna Matata. No, I don't know what it means, but the kids keep talking about it.

11:45 a.m.–12:15 p.m. Sprawl. When it gets too tiring to hold my head up, assume the sprawl: full out on back, paws sticking out in four directions. Petting is assured. But don't fall asleep. Fall asleep, and you're vulnerable to a belly wrestle attack. I hate the belly wrestle attack.

12:15–12:30 p.m. Lunch in the Staff Room. Anybody got yogurt? No? Then never mind.

12:30–1:00 p.m. Cart Ride! When the afternoon clerks shelve books, jump on the cart and hitch a ride around the library. Oh, man, it's relaxing to go completely limp and let my legs hang down between the bars of the metal rack.

1:00–3:55 p.m. Afternoon Free Time. See how the day is going. Mix in a trip up to the lights with more lap time. Greet the afternoon crowd. Spend ten minutes with Mom. Fur licking is encouraged, not mandatory. And don't forget to find a nice box to nap in. As if it's possible to forget that!

3:55 p.m. Dinner. They keep thinking dinnertime is four o'clock. If I sit here long enough, they'll eventually learn.

4:55 p.m. Mom Leaves. Jump around so she'll remember you want to play. A running jump off a bookshelf, complete with somersault, works every time.

5:30 p.m. Play. Mom calls it Boodha track. I call it the ball thingy because there's nothing better than batting that ball around that track. Except for my red yarn. I absolutely love my red yarn. Does anyone want to dangle it for me?

8:55 p.m. Last Shift Leaves. Repeat 4:55 routine, but don't expect the same results unless Joy's working the night shift. Joy always finds time to wad up paper and toss it across the library. Sprint after the paper as fast as possible, but once you get there, always ignore it.

9:00 p.m.–7:30 a.m. My Time! None of your business, nosy.

17

Dewey in the Modern World

I'm not naïve. I know not everyone in Spencer embraced Dewey. For instance, that woman still wrote regular letters threatening to bring her cow downtown if the city didn't stop the injustice, the horror, of a cat living in a public building. She was the most vocal, but she certainly wasn't the only person who didn't understand the Dewey phenomenon.

'What's so special about that cat?' they would say over a cup of coffee at Sister's Café. 'He never leaves the library. He sleeps a lot. He doesn't *do* anything.'

By which they meant Dewey didn't create jobs. Dewey was appearing regularly in magazines, newspapers, and on the radio around the country, but he wasn't improving our municipal parks. He wasn't paving roads. He wasn't out recruiting new businesses. The worst of the farm crisis had passed; spirits were rising; it was time for Spencer to spread its wings and attract new employers to our plucky Midwest town fairly far off the beaten track.

The Spencer economic development commission scored its first big triumph in 1992 when Montfort, a large meatpacking company headquartered in Colorado, decided to lease the slaughterhouse on the north end of town. In 1952, when local businessmen developed the property, the plant was the pride of Spencer. It was locally owned, locally run, and employed local workers at top wages. In 1974, the salary was fifteen dollars an hour, the best-paying job in town. Trucks lined up for a mile waiting to be unloaded. The company began packaging several products under a Spencer Foods label. That label was a source of pride, especially when you'd drive to Sioux Falls or down to Des Moines and see the Spencer name in the big new grocery stores.

In 1968, sales started dropping. Processing conglomerates had moved into nearby towns with more efficient plants and cheaper labor. The owners tried to rebrand the products and retool the plant, but nothing worked. In 1978, the Spencer Packing Company was sold to a national competitor. When the workers wouldn't take nonunion wages of five-fifty an hour, the company closed the plant and moved the work to Skylar, Nebraska. Land O'Lakes moved in next, but when the recession hit in the mid-1980s, they closed up and left, too. They didn't have ties to the community, and there was no economic reason to stay.

Ten years later, Montfort negotiated a lease with the absentee owner of the plant. They just needed the building rezoned so they could expand and upgrade it. Small towns all over the country were desperate for jobs, but the jobs that had paid fifteen dollars in 1974 were being offered by Montfort at five dollars an hour with almost no benefits. This was slaughter work, which was physically brutal and psychologically numbing, not to mention smelly, noisy, dirty, and polluting. Locals didn't want the work, at least not for long. Most of the people who ended up in the jobs were Hispanic immigrants. Towns around Spencer with slaughterhouses, such as Storm Lake, were already 25 percent Hispanic, or more.

Still, Montfort had steamrolled through dozens of towns, and they didn't even bother addressing our concerns or offering concessions. The town leaders were for the plant, why worry about the citizens? The city council offered the usual public forum on the proposed zoning changes. The forum usually took place in front of five people in a little room at the council offices. The demand was so great this time that they held this debate in the largest room in town, the middle school gym. Three thousand people showed up that night, more than 25 percent of the town. It wasn't much of a debate.

'Slaughterhouses are messy. What are they going to do about the waste?'

'Slaughterhouses are loud. That factory is only a mile from downtown.'

'Don't even get me started on the smell.'

'What about the hog trucks? Will they come straight down Grand Avenue? Has anybody thought about the traffic?'

'We want local jobs. How are these jobs going to benefit our city?'

Outside of the economic development commission and the city council, there weren't a hundred people in that gymnasium who supported the slaughterhouse. The next day, the zoning change was voted down.

Some people – Montfort supporters in the city and economic development boards in nearby towns – hinted that the decision was racially motivated. 'Lily-white Spencer,' they snickered, 'doesn't want Mexicans moving in.'

I don't believe that at all. Spencer is not a racist town. In the 1970s, for instance, we welcomed one hundred refugee families from Laos. It's true we looked at the changes in towns like Storm Lake and Worthington and didn't like what we saw, but the problem was the slaughterhouses themselves, not the workers. Spencer banded together that day not against immigrants but against pollution, traffic, and environmental disaster. We weren't willing to sell our way of life for two hundred of the worst jobs in the country. If we did, it meant we had learned nothing from Land O'Lakes, who walked out of that very building when we needed them most. Maybe, as some suggested, we were turning our backs on economic progress to preserve the kind of town – a town based on local merchants, farmers, and small manufacturers – that can no longer survive in modern America. All I know is this: Spencer would be a different town if the first thing you saw (and smelled and heard) when you drove in from the north was a slaughterhouse, and I think we're better without it.

Spencer is not antibusiness. Within a year, the old slaughterhouse was turned into a refrigerated storage facility. Storage didn't provide as many jobs, but the wages were better and you didn't get pollution, noise, or traffic. You barely even noticed it was there.

Two years later, in 1994, Spencer welcomed with open arms what many consider the biggest, baddest conglomerate on the block: Wal-Mart. The downtown merchants were against Wal-Mart, especially a Wal-Mart superstore, so they brought in a consultant to advise them. After all, local businesses had carried this town. Why should they turn over what they had invested in and built to a national competitor?

'Wal-Mart will be the best thing to ever happen to the businesses in Spencer,' the consultant told them. 'If you try to compete with them, you will lose. But if you find a niche they aren't serving, for instance by providing specialty products or knowledgeable, hands-on service, you will win. Why? Because Wal-Mart will bring more customers to town. It's that simple.'

The consultant was right. There were losers, most obviously Shopko, which packed up and left town, but business at the downtown merchants has increased significantly since Wal-Mart arrived. Wal-Mart did what the railroad depot had done decades before: it made Spencer a regional destination.

The same year, 1994, the Spencer Public Library entered the modern era. Out went the antiquated book-management system, with its cards, stamps, catalog drawers, checkout bins, late-notice slips, complex filing systems, and of course, dozens and dozens of boxes. In came a fully automated system complete with eight computers. The bins for the cards, where Dewey loved to lounge in the afternoon, were replaced with a circulation computer. Kim's typewriter, which Dewey had loved as a kitten, fell silent and motionless. We threw a party, pulled all the drawers out of our card catalogs, dumped thousands of cards on the floor, then turned on the one public-access computer that would replace them all. The three card catalog cabinets, with their hundreds of tiny drawers, were sold at auction. I bought one for my house. I keep it in my basement with a 1950s flip-top desk from the Moneta School. The card catalog holds all my craft supplies; the desk holds all Jodi's papers and artwork from elementary school, which I've kept carefully preserved for thirty years.

After the technology update of 1994, people began using the library differently. Before computers, if a student was assigned a report on monkeys, she checked out every book we had on monkeys. Now she did research online and checked out one book. Patron visits to the Spencer Library rose between 1994 and 2006, but only a third as many books were checked out. In 1987, when Dewey arrived, it was common for the book drop to overflow with books. We haven't had a full drop box in a decade. Our most popular items for checkout are classic movies on DVD – the local video stores don't carry them – and video games. We have nineteen computers for public use, sixteen with Internet access. Even though we're small, we are tenth in the number of computers available to patrons in the entire Iowa library system.

A librarian clerk's job used to involve filing and answering reference questions. Now it's understanding computers and inputting data. To keep track of usage, the clerk working the circulation desk used to make a hash mark on a piece of paper every time a patron entered the library. You can imagine how accurate that system was, especially when the library was busy and the clerk was answering reference questions. Now we have an electronic clicker that records every person who comes through the door. The checkout system tells us exactly how many books, games, and movies come and go and tracks which items are the most popular and which haven't been touched in years.

And yet, for all that, the Spencer Public Library remains essentially the same. The carpet is different. The back window, which looked out on the alley, has been plastered over and covered with bookshelves. There's less wood, fewer drawers, and more electronics. But there are still children's groups laughing and listening to stories. Middle school students killing time. Older people thumbing through the newspaper. Businessmen reading magazines. This library has never been Carnegie's quiet cathedral to knowledge, but it's still a relaxed, and relaxing, place.

And when you walk into the library, you still notice the books: shelf after shelf and row after row of books. The covers may be more colorful, the art more expressive, and the type more contemporary, but in general the books look the same as they did in 1982, and 1962, and 1942. And that's not going to change. Books have survived television, radio, talking pictures, circulars (early magazines), dailies (early newspapers), Punch and Judy shows, and Shakespeare's plays. They have survived World War II, the Hundred Years' War, the Black Death, and the fall of the Roman Empire. They even survived the Dark Ages, when almost no one could read and each book had to be copied by hand. They aren't going to be killed off by the Internet.

And neither is the library. We may not be the soothingly silent book depository of yesteryear, but we serve the community better than ever. We are connected to the wider world like never before. We can order any book at any time; we research at the touch of a button; we communicate on an electronic bulletin board with other librarians, swapping tips and information essential to making each library better and more efficient; and we access hundreds of newspapers and magazines for less than the cost of ten subscriptions only ten years ago. The number of people entering the Spencer Public Library keeps rising. Does it matter if they are checking out books, renting movies, playing video games, or visiting a cat?

Dewey didn't care about any of that, of course. He always focused on the here and now. And he loved the new library. Sure, he lost a few boxes, but there are always boxes in a library that orders books on an almost daily basis. Computers may seem cold compared to the old hands-on system of wood, paper, and ink, but to Dewey they were warm. Literally. He loved to sit on them and bask in the heat of their exhaust. I took a picture of him up there, which became the image on our new computerized checkout cards. The company that made the cards loved it. Every time I went to a library convention, I would see Dewey emblazoned on a huge banner above their booth.

Almost as good, at least from Dewey's perspective, were the new sensor posts beside the front door, which beeped if you tried to leave without checking out your library materials. Dewey's new favorite position was just inside the left post. (Just like the left shoulder for the Dewey Carry. Was Dewey left-pawed?) He sat by that post for the first hour of every day, starting promptly at two minutes to nine. With Dewey and the posts crowding the entranceway, there was almost no space for patrons to walk. Before, it was difficult to ignore Dewey when he was in front-door greeting mode; with the new sensors, it was impossible.

BASIC RULES FOR CATS WHO HAVE A LIBRARY TO RUN
(according to Dewey Readmore Books)

First printed in the
Library Cat Society newsletter,
and since reprinted
numerous times
around the world.

1. STAFF: If you are feeling particularly lonely and wanting more attention from the staff, sit on whatever papers, project, or computer they happen to be working on at the time – but sit with your back to the person and act aloof, so as not to appear too needy. Also, be sure to continually rub against the leg of the staff person who is wearing dark brown, blue, or black for maximum effect.

2. PATRONS: No matter how long the patron plans on staying at the library, climb into their briefcase or book bag for a long comfortable sleep until they must dump you out on the table in order to leave.

3. LADDERS: Never miss an opportunity to climb on ladders. It does not matter which human is on the ladder. It only matters that you get to the top and stay there.

4. CLOSING TIME: Wait until ten minutes before closing time to get up from your nap. Just as the staff is getting ready to turn out the lights and lock the door, do all your cutest tricks in an effort to get them to stay and play with you. (Although this doesn't work very often, sometimes they can't resist giving in to one short game of hide-and-seek.)

5. BOXES: Your humans must realize that all boxes that enter the library are yours. It doesn't matter how large, how small, or how full the box should be, it is yours! If you cannot fit your entire body into the box, then use whatever part of your body fits to assume ownership for naptime. (I have used one or two paws, my head, or even just my tail to gain entry and each works equally well for a truly restful sleep.)

6. MEETINGS: No matter the group, timing, or subject matter, if there is a meeting scheduled in the meeting room, you have an obligation to attend. If they have shut you out by closing the door, cry pitifully until they let you in or until someone opens the door to use the restroom or get a drink of water. After you gain entry, be sure to go around the room and greet each attendee. If there is a film or slide show, climb on any table close to the screen, settle in, and watch the film to conclusion. As the credits roll, feign extreme boredom and leave the meeting before it concludes.

And the library cat's golden rule for all time . . .

Never forget, nor let humans forget, that you own the joint!

18

Puss in Books

The computers weren't the only change in Dewey's life. Crystal, Dewey's friend from the special education class, graduated and began a life I can't imagine, but one I pray was happy. The little girl who had been afraid of Dewey overcame her fear of cats. She still approached the desk sometimes and asked us to lock Dewey up, but now she said it with a smile. Like any ten-year-old, she liked having adults do what she asked. The other children her age, the ones Dewey had spent Story Hour with that first year, were growing up, too. The middle school kids who had rolled pencils at him were leaving. He had been in the library six years, and it was inevitable that many of the children he had known were moving away or moving on.

Jean Hollis Clark, my assistant director, left for a new job. Eventually she was replaced by Kay Larson, whom I had known for years. Kay was laid-back and practical, a strong Iowa farm woman. She had been a chemical engineer and worked on oil rigs in the Gulf before marrying a farmer and moving back to Iowa. There were no engineering jobs in the area, so she did slaughter work for a time before landing a position at the tiny library in Petersen, about thirty miles south of Spencer. Maybe I should say *the* position, since the Petersen Library was a one-person show.

I hired Kay because she was good with computers, and we needed someone who could keep up with new technology. I also knew she was a cat person. In fact, twenty cats lived in her barn, as well as two in her house. 'Typical tomcat,' she'd say with Iowa practicality whenever Dewey copped a little attitude or refused to engage in a patron's two-armed hug. She thought Dewey was smart and beautiful, but she didn't think he was anything that special.

But Dewey never lacked for friends. Tony, our painter, scratched the Dewkster whenever he came to see his wife, Sharon, who was expecting their third child. It was an unplanned pregnancy, but it made them both happy. Sharon called from the hospital the day of the birth. She was crying. 'Emmy has Down syndrome,' she said. She had never suspected anything was wrong, and the surprise was shattering.

Sharon took a few months off from the library, and by the time she came back she was head over heels in love with Emmy.

Dewey's old friend Doris Armstrong still brought him little gifts and surprises, and she loved to dangle his beloved red Christmas yarn while he jumped with delight. She was as gregarious and charming as ever, but shortly after the library remodel she began to have severe attacks of vertigo. The doctors couldn't determine the cause, so they guessed panic attacks. Then her hands began to tremble, and eventually she could barely put the covers on books. She no longer trusted herself to pet Dewey, but he didn't mind. The more she trembled, the more he brushed his back against her arm and lounged on her desk to keep her company.

Then one morning Dewey ran into my office crying. This was unusual, but he was leading me toward his food bowl so I thought he wanted a snack. Instead, I found Doris lying on the floor of the staff room. She was having such a severe vertigo attack she couldn't stand up. For days, she could barely eat she was so dizzy. The next time I found her on the floor, she not only had vertigo, but was sure she was having a heart attack. A few months later, Doris found a tiny black kitten. She brought the kitten to the library and, with trembling hands, held it out for me to hold. I could feel its heart racing and its lungs gasping for air. The kitten was weak, frightened, and sick.

'What should I do?' she asked me. I didn't know.

The next day Doris came into the library crying. She had taken the kitten home with her, and it had died during the night. Sometimes a cat is more than an animal, and sometimes the loss you mourn is not just the obvious one. Dewey sat with Doris the whole day, and she even managed to lay her hands on him and pet him, but his presence didn't soothe her. Not long after, Doris retired from the library and moved away to be near her family in Minnesota.

And yet, despite the changes, Dewey's life stayed essentially the same. Children grew up, but there were always new ones turning four. Staffers moved on, but even on our skimpy budget we managed new hires. Dewey may never again have had a friend like Crystal, but he still met the special education class at the door every week. He even developed relationships with patrons like Mark Carey, who owned the electronics store on the corner. Dewey knew Mark wasn't a cat lover, and he took fiendish delight in suddenly jumping on the table and scaring the bejeebers out of him. Mark took delight in kicking Dewey out of whatever chair he was lounging in, even if there was nobody else in the library.

One morning I noticed a businessman in a suit sitting at a table, reading the *Wall Street Journal*. It looked like he had stopped in to kill time before a meeting, so I wasn't expecting to see a fluffy orange tail sticking out at his side. I looked closer and saw that Dewey had plopped down on one page of his newspaper. Busy. Businessman. On his way to a meeting. 'Oh, Dewey,' I thought, 'you're pushing it now.' Then I realized the man was holding the newspaper with his right hand while petting Dewey with his left. One of them was purring; the other was smiling. That's when I knew Dewey and the town had fallen into a comfort zone, that the general outline of our lives had been set, at least for the next few years.

Maybe that's why I was so surprised when I arrived at the library one morning to find Dewey pacing. He was never agitated like that; even my presence didn't calm him. When I opened the door, he ran a few steps, then stopped, waiting for me to follow.

'Do you need to go to the bathroom, Dewey? You know you don't have to wait for me.'

It wasn't the bathroom, and he didn't have any interest in breakfast, either. He kept pacing back and forth, crying for me. Dewey never cried unless he was in pain, but I knew Dewey. He wasn't in pain.

I tried fixing his food. Nope. I checked to see if he had poop stuck in his fur. Poop in his fur drove him absolutely nuts. I checked his nose to see if he had a temperature, and his ears to see if he had an infection. Nothing.

'Let's make the rounds, Dew.'

Like all felines, Dewey had hair balls. Whenever it happened, our fanatically neat cat was mortified. But he had never acted this strangely, so I braced myself for the mother of all hair balls. I worked my way through fiction and nonfiction, checking every corner. But I didn't find anything.

Dewey was waiting for me in the children's library. The poor cat was in knots. But I didn't find anything there, either.

'I'm sorry, Dewey. I don't understand what you're trying to tell me.'

When the staff arrived, I told them to keep an eye on Dewey. I was extremely busy, and I couldn't spend all morning playing charades with a cat. If Dewey was still acting strange in a few hours, I decided to take him to see Dr. Esterly. I knew he would love that.

Two minutes after the library opened, Jackie Shugars came back to my office. 'You're not going to believe this, Vicki, but Dewey just peed on the cards.'

I jumped up. 'It can't be!'

The library automation wasn't yet complete. To check out a book, we still stamped two cards. One went home with you in the book; the other went into a big bin with hundreds of other cards. When you returned the book, we pulled that card and put the book back on the shelf. Actually there were two bins, one on each side of the front desk. Sure enough, Dewey had peed in the front right corner of one of them.

I wasn't mad at Dewey. I was worried about him. He'd been in the library for years; he'd never acted out. This was completely out of character. But I didn't have long to think the situation through before one of our regular patrons came up and whispered in my ear, 'You better get down here, Vicki. There's a bat in the children's department.'

Sure enough, there was the bat, hanging by his heels behind a ceiling beam. And there was Dewey at *my* heels.

I tried to tell you. I tried to tell you. Now look what you've done. You've let a patron find it. We could have taken care of this before anyone arrived. Now there are children in the library. I thought you were protecting them.

Have you ever been lectured by a cat? It's not a pleasant experience. Especially when the cat is right. And especially when a bat is involved. I hate bats. I couldn't stand the thought of having one in the library, and I couldn't imagine being trapped all night with that thing flying all over the place. Poor Dewey.

'Don't worry, Dewey. Bats sleep during the day. He won't hurt anybody.'

Dewey didn't look convinced, but I couldn't worry about that now. I didn't want to scare the patrons, especially the children, so I quietly called the city hall janitor and told him, 'Get down to the library right away. And bring your ladder.'

He climbed up for a look. 'It's a bat, all right.'

'Shhh. Keep your voice down.'

He climbed down. 'You got a vacuum cleaner?'

I shivered. 'Don't use the vacuum cleaner.'

'How about Tupperware? Something with a lid.'

I just stared at him. This was disgusting.

Someone said, 'We've got an empty coffee can. It's got a lid.'

The ordeal was over in a matter of seconds. Thank goodness. Now I had to sort out the mess in the cards.

'This is my fault,' I told Jackie, who was still manning the circulation desk.

'I know.' Jackie has a droll sense of humor.

'Dewey was trying to warn us. I'll clean this up.'

'I figured you would.'

I pulled out about twenty cards. Underneath them was a big pile of bat guano. Dewey hadn't just been trying to get my attention; he'd been using his scent glands to cover the stench of the intruder.

'Oh, Dewey, you must think I'm so stupid.'

The next morning, Dewey started what I referred to as his sentry phase. Each morning, he sniffed three heating vents: the one in my office, the one by the front door, and the one by the children's library. He sniffed each one again after lunch. He knew those vents led somewhere and that therefore they were access points. He had taken it upon himself to use his powerful nose to protect us, to be our proverbial canary in the coal mine. His attitude was, *If you can't even figure out there's a bat in the library, how are you going to take care of all these people?*

I suppose there could be something funny about such a vigilant cat. What was Dewey worried about, a terrorist attack on the Spencer Public Library? Call me sentimental, but I found it very endearing. At one point in his life, Dewey wasn't content until he expanded his world to the street outside the library. Now that his story had gone all over the country, he wanted nothing more than to hunker down in the library and protect his friends. You would have to love a cat like that, right?

And the world apparently did, because Dewey's fame continued to grow. He was featured in all the cat magazines – *Cats, Cat Fancy, Cats & Kittens*. If the magazine had *cat* in the title, Dewey was probably in it. He even appeared in *Your Cat*, a leading publication of the British feline press. Marti Attoun, a young freelance writer, traveled to Spencer with a photographer. Her article appeared in *American Profile*, a weekend insert featured in more than a thousand newspapers. Then, in the summer of 1996, a documentary filmmaker from Boston turned up in out-of-the-way Spencer, Iowa, camera in tow, ready to put Dewey in his first movie.

Gary Roma was traveling the country, from the East Coast to North Dakota, to create a documentary about library cats. He arrived expecting the kind of footage he'd shot at other libraries: cats darting apprehensively behind bookshelves, walking away, sleeping, and doing everything possible to avoid looking into the camera. Dewey was exactly the opposite. He didn't ham it up, but he went about all his usual activities, and he performed them on command. Gary arrived early in the morning to catch Dewey waiting for me at the front door. He shot Dewey sitting by the sensor posts greeting patrons; lying in his Buddha pose; playing with his favorite toys, Marty Mouse and the red yarn; sitting on a patron's shoulder in the Dewey Carry; and sleeping in a box.

Gary said, 'This is the best footage I've shot so far. If you don't mind, I'll come back after lunch.'

After lunch I sat down for an interview. After a few introductory questions, Gary asked, 'What is the meaning of Dewey?'

I told him, 'Dewey's great for the library. He relieves stress. He makes it feel like home. People love him, especially children.'

'Yes, but what's the deeper meaning?'

'There is no deeper meaning. Everyone enjoys spending time with Dewey. He makes us happy. He's one of us. What more to life is there than that?'

He kept pressing for meaning, meaning, meaning. Gary's first film was *Off the Floor & Off the Wall: A Doorstop Documentary*, and I could imagine him pressing all his subjects: 'What does your doorstop mean to you?'

'It keeps the door from hitting the wall.'

'Yes, but what about the deeper meaning?'

'Well, I can use it to hold the door open.'

'Go deeper.'

'Umm, it keeps the room drafty?'

Gary must have gotten deeper meaning out of doorstops because one review mentions linguists dissecting the etymology of the word and philosophers musing about a world without doors.

About six months after filming, in the winter of 1997, we threw a party for the inaugural showing of *Puss in Books*. The library was packed. The film started with a distant shot of Dewey sitting on the floor of the Spencer library waving his tail slowly back and forth. As the camera zoomed in and followed him under a table, across some shelves, and finally to his favorite cart for a ride, you heard my voice in the background: 'We arrived at work one morning, and we went back to open the book drop and empty the books out, and there inside was this tiny little kitten. He was buried under tons of books, the book drop was just full of books. People will come in, and they'll hear the story of how we acquired Dewey, and they'll say, "Oh, you poor little thing. You were thrown into that book drop on that day." And I'll say, "Poor little thing, my foot. That was the luckiest day of that boy's life, because he's king around here, and he knows it."'

As the last words rolled out, Dewey stared right into the camera, and boy, could you tell I was right. He really was the king.

By this time, I was used to strange calls about Dewey. The library was getting a couple requests a week for interviews, and articles about our famous cat were turning up in our mail on an almost weekly basis. Dewey's official photograph, the one taken by Rick Krebsbach just after Jodi left Spencer, had appeared in magazines, newsletters, books, and newspapers from Minneapolis, Minnesota, to Jerusalem, Israel. It even appeared in a cat calendar; Dewey was Mr. January. But even I was surprised to receive a phone call from the Iowa office of a national pet food company.

'We've been watching Dewey,' they said, 'and we're impressed.' Who wouldn't be? 'He seems like an extraordinary cat. And obviously people love him.' You don't say! 'We'd like to use him in a print advertising campaign. We can't offer money, but we will provide free cat food for life.'

I have to admit, I was tempted. Dewey was a finicky eater, and we were indulgent parents. We were throwing out dishes full of food every day just because he didn't like the smell, and we were donating a hundred cans of out-of-favor cat food a year. Since the Feed the Kitty campaign of loose change and soda cans didn't cover the costs and I had vowed to never use a penny of city funds for Dewey's care, most of that money was coming out of my pocket. I was personally subsidizing the feeding of a good portion of the cats in Spencer.

'I'll talk to the library board.'

'We'll send over samples.'

By the time the next library board meeting rolled around, the decision had already been made. Not by me or the board, but by Dewey himself. Mr. Finicky completely rejected the free samples.

Are you kidding me? he told me with a disdainful sniff. *I can't shill for this junk.*

'I'm sorry,' I told the manufacturer. 'Dewey only eats Fancy Feast.'

19

The World's Worst Eater

Dewey's pickiness wasn't just a matter of personality. He had a disease. No, really, it's true. As far as digestive systems were concerned, that cat really got a lemon.

Dewey always hated being petted on the stomach. Stroke his back, scratch his ears, even pull his tail and poke him in the eye, but never pet his stomach. I didn't think much of it until Dr. Esterly tried to clean his anal glands when he was about two years old. 'I just push down on the glands and squeeze them clean,' he explained. 'It will take thirty seconds.'

Sounded easy enough. I held Dewey while Dr.
Esterly prepared his equipment, which consisted of a
pair of gloves and a paper towel. 'Nothing to it, Dewey,'
I whispered. 'It will be over before you know it.'

But as soon as Dr. Esterly pressed down, Dewey
screamed. This wasn't a mild complaint. This was
a full-fledged, terrified cry that ripped out from the
base of his stomach. His body bolted like it had been
hit by lightning, and his legs scrambled frantically.
Then he threw his mouth over my finger and bit
down. Hard.

Dr. Esterly looked at my finger. 'He shouldn't have
done that.'

I rubbed the sore. 'It's not a problem.'

'Yes, it is a problem. A cat shouldn't bite like that.'

I wasn't worried. That wasn't Dewey. I knew Dewey;
he wasn't a biter. And I could still see the panic in the
poor cat's eyes. He wasn't looking at anything. He
was just staring. The pain had been blinding.

After that, Dewey hated Dr. Esterly. He even hated
the thought of getting in the car because it might
lead to Dr. Esterly. As soon as we pulled into the
veterinary office's parking lot, he started shaking.
The smell of the lobby sent him into uncontrollable
tremors. He would bury his head in the crook of my
arm as if to say, *Protect me.*

As soon as he heard Dr. Esterly's voice, Dewey
growled. Many cats hate the veterinarian in his office
but treat him as any other human in the outside world.
Not Dewey. He feared Dr. Esterly unconditionally. If

he heard his voice in the library, Dewey growled and sprinted to the other side of the room. If Dr. Esterly managed to sneak up on him and reached out to pet him, Dewey sprang up, looked around in panic, and bolted away. I think he recognized Dr. Esterly's smell. That hand, to Dewey, was the hand of death. He had found his archenemy, and it happened to be one of the nicest men in town.

A few uneventful years went by after the anal gland incident, but Dewey eventually went back to prowling for rubber bands. As a kitten, his rubber band hunting had been half-hearted, and he was easily distracted. At about five years of age, Dewey became serious. I started finding the sticky remnants on the floor almost every morning. His litter box was filled not only with rubber worms but with the occasional drop of blood. Sometimes Dewey came tearing out of the back room like someone had lit a firecracker under his rear end.

Dr. Esterly diagnosed Dewey with constipation. Extreme constipation. 'What kind of food does Dewey eat?'

I rolled my eyes. Dewey was well on his way to becoming the world's worst eater. 'He's very picky. He has a remarkable sense of smell, so he can tell when the food is old or off in some way. Cat food isn't the highest quality, you know. It's just a bunch of leftover animal parts. So you can't blame him.'

Dr. Esterly looked at me like a kindergarten teacher eyeing a parent who had just explained away her child's disruptive behavior. Overindulgent, are we?

'He always eats canned food?'

'Yes.'

'Good. Does he drink much water?'

'Never.'

'Never?'

'The cat avoids his water dish like poison.'

'More water,' Dr. Esterly assured me. 'That should clear up the problem.'

Thanks, Doc, nothing to it. Except have you ever tried to get a cat to drink water against his will? It's impossible.

I started with gentle coaxing. Dewey turned away in disgust.

I tried bribery. 'No food until you drink some water. Don't look at me like that. I can last longer than you can.' But I couldn't. I always gave in.

I started petting Dewey as he ate. Slowly the petting turned to pushing. 'If I force his head down into the water,' I thought, 'he has to drink.' Needless to say, that plan didn't work.

Maybe it was the water. We tried warm water. We tried cold water. We tried refreshing the water every five minutes. We tried different faucets. This was the mid-1990s, so there was no such thing as bottled water, at least not in Spencer, Iowa. We tried putting ice in the water dish. Everyone likes ice water, right? Actually, the ice worked. Dewey took a lick. But otherwise, nothing. How could an animal stay alive without water?

A few weeks later I rounded the corner into the staff bathroom and there was Dewey, on the toilet, his head completely buried in the bowl. All I could see was his rear end sticking straight up in the air. Toilet water! You sneaky son of a gun.

'Well,' I thought, 'at least he isn't going to die of dehydration.'

The door was left open when the staff bathroom was unoccupied, so that toilet was Dewey's primary water source. But he also loved the women's bathroom in the front of the library. Joy DeWall was the library clerk who spent the most time shelving books. Dewey would watch her loading books onto the book cart, then hop on for a ride once it was full. He would stare at the bookshelves as the cart rolled past, and whenever he saw something he liked, he'd signal Joy that he wanted to get off, like he was riding a little cat trolley. He knew she was a soft touch, so he always begged her to let him into that bathroom. Once inside the sanctum, he jumped on the sink and begged for the water to be turned on. He didn't drink this water. He watched it. Something about the way it bounced off the drain plug fascinated him. He could watch that water for an hour, occasionally taking a quick slap at it with his paw.

But that didn't help his constipation, and neither did trips to his royal porcelain bowl. Whether he watched water or drank it, Dewey still couldn't go. When it got really bad, Dewey tended to hide. One morning, poor Sharon Joy reached into the top drawer of the circulation desk for a tissue, but instead grabbed a handful of hair. She literally fell out of her chair.

'How did he get in there?' she asked, staring down at Dewey's back. His head and rear were completely buried in the drawer.

Good question. The drawer hadn't been opened all morning, so Dewey must have climbed in during the night. I poked around under the desk. Sure enough, there was a small opening behind the drawers. But this was the top drawer, more than three feet off the ground. Mr. Rubber Spine had wiggled his way to the top of the crevice and turned a tight corner, all to curl up in a space of no more than a few inches.

I tried to rouse him, but Dewey shrugged me off and didn't move. This wasn't like him at all. Obviously something was wrong.

As I suspected, Dewey was constipated. Extremely constipated. Again. This time, Dr. Esterly performed a thorough exam, with lots of deep poking and prodding of Dewey's sensitive belly. Oh, it was painful to watch. This was definitely the end of the cat-doctor relationship.

'Dewey has megacolon.'

'You're going to have to walk me through that, Doctor.'

'Dewey's colon is distended. This causes his intestinal contents to pool inside his body cavity.'

Silence.

'Dewey's colon is permanently stretched out. This allows it to store more waste. By the time Dewy tries to get rid of it, the opening to the outside world is too small.'

'A little extra water isn't going to solve the problem, is it?'

'I'm afraid there's no cure. The condition is rare.' In fact, they weren't even sure of the cause. Apparently, distended feline colons were not a top research priority.

If Dewey had lived in the alley, his megacolon would have shortened his life. In a controlled environment like the library, I could expect periodic but severe bouts of constipation, accompanied by very picky eating. When the plumbing tends to back up, cats get awfully choosy about what they put in the system. See, I told you he had a disease.

Dr. Esterly suggested an expensive cat food, the kind you could buy only from a veterinarian. I forget the name, maybe Laboratory Diet, Middle-aged Cat with Bowel Troubles Formula? The bill almost broke the budget. I hated to dish out thirty dollars for something I knew wasn't going to work.

I told Dr. Esterly, 'Dewey's a picky eater. He's not going to like this.'

'Put it in his bowl. Don't give him anything else. He'll eat it. No cat will starve itself to death.' As I was packing up to leave, he added, as much to himself as to me, 'We're going to have to watch Dewey carefully. There will be ten thousand unhappy people if something happens to him.'

'There will be more people than that, Dr. Esterly. A lot more.'

I put the fancy new food in the bowl. Dewey didn't eat it. He sniffed it once and walked away.

This food, it's no good. I want the usual, please.

The next day, he dropped the subtle approach. Instead of sniffing and walking away, he sat down by the food bowl and cried.

Whhhyyyy? What have I done to deserve this?

'Sorry, Dewey. Doctor's orders.'

After two days, he was weak, but he didn't waver. He hadn't even batted the food with his paw. That's when I realized Dewey was stubborn. Painfully stubborn. He was a mellow cat. He was accommodating. But when it came to an important principle like food, Dewey would never roll over and play dog.

And neither would I. Mom could be stubborn, too.

So Dewey went behind my back to the rest of the staff. First he hit up Sharon by jumping on her desk and rubbing her arm. He had taken to sitting on Sharon's desk and watching her eat lunch, and she seemed appreciative of a good meal.

When that didn't work, he tried his old friend Joy, always a soft touch. Then he tried Audrey, Cynthia, Paula, everybody, right down the line. He tried Kay, even though he knew she was the no-nonsense, practical type. Kay had no time for weakness. But I could see even she was beginning to waver. She tried to act tough, but she was developing a real warm spot in her heart for the Dew.

I didn't care, let them disapprove. I was going to win this round. It might break my heart now, but in the end Dewey would thank me. And besides, I was Mommy, and I said so!

On the fourth day, even the patrons turned on me. 'Just feed him, Vicki! He's so hungry.' Dewey had been shamelessly putting on a starving cat act for his fans, and it had clearly been working.

Finally, on the fifth day, I caved and gave Dewey his favorite can of Fancy Feast. He gobbled it down without even coming up for air. *That's it*, he said, licking his lips and then stepping to the corner for a long tongue bath of his face and ears. *We all feel better now, don't we?*

That night I went out and bought him an armful of cans. I couldn't fight anymore. 'Better a constipated cat,' I thought, 'than a dead one.'

For two months Dewey was happy. I was happy. All was right with the world.

Then Dewey decided he didn't like Fancy Feast, chunky chicken flavor. He wasn't going to eat another bite of it. He wanted something new, and make it snappy, thank you very much. I bought a new flavor, something in the moist smelly blob category. Dewey took one sniff and walked away. *Nope, not that one, either.*

'You'll eat it, young man, or no dessert for you.'

At the end of the day, the food was still there, dried out and crusty. What was I supposed to do? The cat was sick! It took five tries, but I found a flavor he liked. It only lasted a few weeks. Then he wanted something new. Oh, brother. I hadn't just ceded the battlefield; I'd completely lost the war.

By 1997 the situation was completely absurd. How could you not laugh at an entire bookshelf full of cans of cat food? I'm not exaggerating. We kept Dewey's items on two shelves in the staff area, and one of them was only for food. We had at least five flavors on hand at all times. The Dew had midwestern taste. His favorite flavors were beef, chunky chicken, beef & liver, and turkey, but you never knew when another flavor would strike his fancy. He hated seafood, but he fell in love with shrimp. For a week. Then he wouldn't touch it.

Unfortunately Dewey was still constipated, so on Dr. Esterly's orders I copied a page out of a calendar and hung it on the wall. Every time someone found a present in Dewey's litter box, they marked the date. The calendar was known throughout the office as Dewey's Poop Chart.

I can only imagine what someone like Sharon thought. She was very funny, and she loved Dewey, but she was also fastidious. Now we were discussing poop on a regular basis. She must have thought I was nuts. But she marked that chart, and she never complained. Of course, Dewey only pooped a couple times a week, so we weren't exactly wearing down the nibs of our pens.

When Dewey hadn't gone for three days, we locked him in the back closet for a romantic date with his litter. Dewey hated being locked anywhere, especially a closet. I hated it almost as much as Dewey, especially in the winter because the closet was unheated.

'It's for your own good, Dew.'

After a half hour, I let him out. If no evidence turned up in the litter box, I gave him an hour to roam and then locked him in for another half hour. No poop, back in the box. Three times was the limit. After three times, he wasn't holding out, he really couldn't go.

This strategy completely backfired. Dewey soon became so pampered he refused to use the bathroom unless someone took him to the box. He stopped going completely at night, which meant first thing in the morning I had to carry him – yes, carry him – to his litter. Talk about being the king!

I know, I know. I was a sucker. A spoiler of cats. But what could I do? I knew how bad Dewey felt. Not just because I had a connection with him, but because I was no stranger to lifelong illness. I'd been in and out of the hospital more times than most doctors. I'd been medevaced to Sioux Falls twice. And I had been through the Mayo Clinic for irritable bowel syndrome, hyperthyroidism, severe migraines, and Graves' disease, among others. At one point I had hives on my legs for two years. It turned out I was allergic to the prayer kneeler at church. A year later I suddenly froze. I couldn't move for half an hour. The staff had to carry me to a car, drive me home, and lay me out in bed. It happened again at a wedding. I had a forkful of wedding cake halfway to my mouth and I couldn't put my arm down. I couldn't even move my tongue to tell anyone. Thank God my friend Faith was there. The cause turned out to be a sudden, severe drop in blood pressure exacerbated by one of my medications.

But worst, by far, were the lumps in my breasts. Even now, I don't feel entirely comfortable talking about it. I've shared this experience with very few people, and it's difficult to break that silence. I don't want anyone to look at me as less than a complete woman or, even worse, some kind of fraud.

Of all the things in my life – the alcoholic husband, the welfare, the surprise hysterectomy – my double mastectomy was by far the hardest. The worst part wasn't the procedure, although it was probably the most physically painful thing I've ever endured. The worst part was the decision. I agonized over it for more than a year. I traveled to Sioux City, Sioux Falls, and Omaha, more than three hours away, to consult physicians, but I couldn't make up my mind.

Mom and Dad encouraged me to have the procedure. They said, 'You have to do it. You have to get healthy. Your life is at stake.'

I talked to my friends, who had helped me through the end of my marriage and so many problems since, but for the first time they didn't talk back. They couldn't deal with it, they admitted later. Breast cancer hit too close to the bone.

I needed to have the surgery. I knew that. If I didn't, it was only a matter of time before I heard the word *cancer*. But I was a single woman. I dated fairly regularly, if not particularly successfully. My friend Bonnie and I still laugh about the Cowboy, whom I met at a dance in West Okoboji. We met up in Sioux City, and he took me to one of those country places with sawdust on the floor. I can't tell you about the food because a fight broke out, someone pulled a knife, and I spent twenty minutes huddled in the women's bathroom. The Cowboy graciously took me back to his house and showed me – I kid you not – how to make bullets. On the way back, he drove me through the stockyards. He found it romantic to see the holding pens in the moonlight.

And yet despite the flops, I still hoped for the right man. I didn't want that hope to die. But who could love me without my breasts? It wasn't losing my sexuality I was worried about. It was losing my femininity, my identity as a woman, my self-image. My parents didn't understand; my friends were too scared to help. What could I do?

One morning there was a knock on my office door. It was a woman I had never met. She came in, closed the door, and said, 'You don't know me, but I'm a patient of Dr. Kolegraff's. He sent me to see you. Five years ago, I had a double mastectomy.'

We talked for two hours. I don't remember her name, and I haven't seen her since (she wasn't from Spencer), but I remember every word. We talked about everything – the pain, the procedure, the recovery, but mostly the emotions. Did she still feel like a woman? Was she still herself? What did she see when she looked in the mirror?

When she left, I not only knew the right decision, I was ready to make it.

The double mastectomy was a multistep process. First, they took my breasts. Then they installed temporary implants called expanders. I had ports under my arms – literally tubes that stuck out from my flesh – and every two weeks I received a saline injection to expand the size of my chest and stretch the skin. Unfortunately the dangers of silicone implants exploded into the news during my first weeks of recovery, and the FDA placed a temporary ban on new implants. I ended up keeping my four-week temporary expanders for eight months. I had so much scar tissue under my armpits that I got shooting pains down my sides whenever the barometric pressure changed. For years, Joy asked me every time she saw a dark cloud, 'Vicki, is it going to rain?'

'Yes,' I'd say, 'but not for another thirty minutes.' I could tell when the rain was coming to within ten minutes just by the level of pain. Once it reached crippling, the rain was almost here. Joy and I would laugh, because I was almost always right, but I really just wanted to sit down, right where I was, and cry.

Nobody knew my pain: not my parents, my friends, or my staff. The doctor dug inside my body and scraped out every ounce of flesh he could find. That hollow, sore, scraped-out feeling was always with me, every minute, but sometimes the pain would wash over me so suddenly and so savagely that I would drop to the floor. I was out of the library, on and off, for most of a year. Many of the days I struggled to my desk I knew I shouldn't have been there at all. With Kay in charge, the library could run without me, but I wasn't sure I could run without it. The routine. The company. The feeling of accomplishment. And most of all, Dewey.

Whenever I had needed him in the past, Dewey had always been by my side. He had perched on my computer when I thought life might overwhelm me, and he had sat beside me on the sofa and waited for Jodi to spend time with us. Now he moved from sitting beside me to climbing up, one paw at a time, and sitting on my lap. He stopped walking beside me and started insisting on climbing into my arms. That might seem like a small thing, but it made all the difference to me because, you see, I didn't have anybody to touch. There was a distance between me and the world, and there was no one to hug me, to tell me it was going to be okay. It wasn't just the surgery. For two years, while I agonized over my decision, mourned my loss, and endured the physical pain, Dewey touched me every day. He sat on me. He snuggled in my arms. And when it was over, when I was finally back to something resembling my normal self, he went right back to sitting at my side. Nobody understood what I was going through for those two years; nobody, that is, but Dewey. He seemed to understand that love was constant, but that it could be raised to a higher level when it really mattered.

Every morning since his first week in the library, Dewey had waited for me at the front door. He would stare at me as I approached, then turn and run for his food bowl when I opened the door. Then, on one of the worst mornings of that terrible two years, he started waving. Yes, waving. I stopped and looked at him. He stopped and looked at me, then started waving again.

It happened the next morning, too. And the next. And the next, until finally I understood this was our new routine. For the rest of his life, as soon as Dewey saw my car pull into the parking lot, he started scratching his right paw on the front door. The wave continued as I crossed the street and approached the door. It wasn't frantic. He wasn't meowing or pacing. He was sitting very still and waving at me, as if welcoming me to the library and, at the same time, reminding me he was there. As if I could ever forget. Every morning, Dewey waving at me as I walked toward the library made me feel better: about the job, about life, about myself. If Dewey was waving, everything was all right.

'Good morning, Dewey,' I would say, my heart singing and the library bursting with life, even on the darkest and coldest mornings. I would look down at him and smile. He would rub against my ankle. My buddy. My boy. Then I would cradle him in my arms and carry him to his litter box. How could I deny him that?

20

Dewey's New Friends

On the afternoon of June 7, 1999, I received a phone call from a Dewey fan. 'Vicki, turn on the radio. You're not going to believe this.'

I turned it on to hear 'and now you know . . . the rest of the story.'

Anyone raised on radio knows that sign-off. Paul Harvey's *The Rest of the Story* is one of the most popular programs in the history of radio. Each broadcast relates a minor but telling incident in the life of a well-known person. The gimmick is that you don't know whom Paul Harvey is talking about until his famous closing.

'And that little boy,' he might say, 'the one who so wanted to cut down that cherry tree, grew up to be none other than George Washington, the father of our country. And now you know . . . the rest of the story.'

Now Paul Harvey was telling the story of a cat who inspired a town and became famous around the world . . . and it all started in a library book drop on a cold January morning in a small Iowa town. And now you know . . .

Who cares if nobody from Paul Harvey's staff called to check the facts? Who cares if they didn't know 10 percent of the rest of the story, the part that made Dewey so special? I sat down at the end of the broadcast and thought, 'That's it. Dewey's really made it now.' And then, because I was so used to the unexpected with Dewey, I wondered what was going to happen next.

For years I had gone to the newspaper and the radio station to pass on Dewey news. With Paul Harvey, I decided to hold back. It wasn't that there weren't plenty of Dewey fans. Patrons asked every day for the latest bit of Dewey news. Children ran into the library, eager and smiling, looking for their friend. But good news about Dewey no longer seemed to impress the rest of the town. In fact, I was beginning to worry it was pushing some people away. Dewey, I suspected, might be a little overexposed.

But only in Spencer. The rest of the world still couldn't get enough. In addition to being on several state boards, I was one of six continuing-education instructors in the Iowa library system. I taught the courses using the Iowa Communication Network (ICN), a teleconferencing system connecting libraries, military depots, hospitals, and schools around the state. Every time I sat down in our ICN room to teach the opening class of a course, the first question was, 'Where's Dewey?'

'Yes,' another librarian would pipe up, 'can we see him?'

Fortunately, Dewey attended all meetings in the ICN room. He preferred meetings of actual people, but teleconferences were acceptable, too. I put Dewey on the table and pushed a button so he appeared on viewing screens all over the state. You could probably hear the gasp in Nebraska.

'He's so cute.'

'Do you think my library should get a cat?'

'Only if it's the right cat.' That's what I always told them. 'You can't get just any cat. He has to be special.'

'Special?'

'Calm, patient, dignified, intelligent, and above all, outgoing. A library cat has to love people. It also helps if he's gorgeous and comes with an unforgettable story.' I didn't mention loving, absolutely loving with his whole heart, being the library cat.

'Okay,' I told them eventually. 'Enough fun. Back to censorship and collection development.'

'One more minute. Please. I want my staff to meet Dewey.'

I looked over at my big orange buddy, who was sprawled out in his favorite spot on the table. 'You're loving this, aren't you?'

He gave me an innocent look. *Who, me? I'm just doing my job.*

It wasn't just librarians who loved Dewey. I was working in my office one morning when Kay called me to the front desk. Standing there was a family of four, two young parents and their children.

'This nice family,' Kay said, with barely disguised amazement, 'is from Rhode Island. They've come to meet Dewey.'

The father extended his hand. 'We were in Minneapolis, so we decided to rent a car and drive down. The kids just love Dewey.'

Was this man crazy? Minneapolis was four and half hours away. 'Wonderful,' I said, shaking their hands. 'How did you find out about Dewey?'

'We read about him in *Cats* magazine. We're cat lovers.'

Obviously.

'Okay,' I said, because I couldn't think of anything else. 'Let's go meet him.'

Dewey was, thank goodness, as eager to please as always. He played with the children. He posed for photographs. I showed the little girl the Dewey Carry, and she walked him all around the library on her left shoulder (always the left). I don't know if it was worth the nine-hour round trip, but the family left happy.

'That was weird,' Kay said once the family was gone. 'It sure was. I bet that never happens again.'

It happened again. And again. And again. And again. They came from Utah, Washington, Mississippi, California, Maine, and every other corner of the map. Older couples, younger couples, families. Many were traveling cross-country and drove one hundred, two hundred miles out of their way to stop in Spencer for the day. I can remember many of their faces, but the only names I remember are Harry and Rita Fein's from New York City because after meeting Dewey they sent both a birthday present and a Christmas present of twenty-five dollars every year for food and supplies. I wish I had thought to write down information on the others, but at first it seemed so unlikely more people would ever come. Why bother? By the time we realized the power of Dewey's appeal, visitors were so common they no longer seemed unusual enough to take note of.

How were these people finding out about Dewey? I have no idea. The library never pursued publicity for Dewey. We never contacted a single newspaper, with the exception of the *Spencer Daily Reporter*. We never hired a publicity agent or marketing manager. After Shopko, we never entered Dewey in any contests. We were Dewey's answering service, nothing more. We picked up the phone, and there was another magazine, another television program, another radio station wanting an interview. Or we opened the mail and found an article about Dewey from a magazine we'd never heard of or a newspaper halfway across the country. A week later, another family popped up at the library.

What were these pilgrims expecting to find? A wonderful cat, of course, but there are wonderful cats sitting homeless in every shelter in America. Why come all this way? Was it love, peace, comfort, acceptance, a reminder of the simple joys of life? Did they just want to spend time with a star?

Or were they hoping to find a cat, a library, a town, an experience that was genuine, that wasn't from the past or for the moment, that was different from their lives but somehow familiar? Is that what Iowa is all about? Maybe the heartland isn't just the place in the middle of the country; maybe it's also the place in the middle of your chest.

Whatever they were after, Dewey delivered. The magazine articles and newscasts touched people. We received letters all the time that started, 'I've never written to a stranger before, but I heard Dewey's story and . . .' His visitors, all of them, left smitten. I know this not only because they told me or because I saw their eyes and their smiles but because they went home and told people the story. They showed them the pictures. At first they sent letters to friends and relatives. Later, when the technology caught on, they sent e-mails. Dewey's face, his personality, his story, it all magnified. He received letters from Taiwan, Holland, South Africa, Norway, Australia. He had pen pals in half a dozen countries. A ripple started in a little town in northwest Iowa, and somehow the human network carried it all over the world.

Whenever I think of Dewey's popularity, I think of Jack Manders. Jack is now retired, but when Dewey arrived he was a middle school teacher and the president of our library board. A few years later, when his daughter was accepted at Hope College in Holland, Michigan, Jack found himself attending a reception for the parents of incoming freshmen. As he stood there in an elegant Michigan nightspot slowly sipping a martini, he fell into conversation with a couple from New York City. Eventually they asked where he was from.

'A small town in Iowa you've never heard of.'

'Oh. Is it near Spencer?'

'Actually,' he told them with surprise, 'it is Spencer.'

The couple perked up. 'Do you ever go to the library?'

'All the time. In fact, I'm on the board.'

The charming, well-dressed woman turned to her husband and, with an almost girlish giggle, exclaimed, 'It's Dewey's daddy!'

A similar thing happened to another board member, Mike Baehr, on a cruise in the South Pacific. During the meet and greet, Mike and his wife realized many of their fellow passengers had never even heard of Iowa. At about the same time, they realized cruises had a social hierarchy based on how many cruises you'd been on, and since this was their first cruise, they were at the bottom of the pecking order. Then a woman came up to them and said, 'I hear you're from Iowa. Do you know Dewey, the library cat?' What an icebreaker! Mike and Peg were off the outcast list, and Dewey was the talk of the cruise.

This is not to say everyone knew Dewey. No matter how famous and popular Dewey became, there was always someone with no idea Spencer Public Library had a cat. A family would drive from Nebraska to see Dewey. They would bring gifts, spend two hours playing with him, taking pictures, talking with the staff. Ten minutes after they left, someone would come up to the desk, obviously worried, and whisper, 'I don't want to alarm you, but I just saw a cat in the building.'

'Yes,' we would whisper back. 'He lives here. He's the world's most famous library cat.'

'Oh,' they'd say with a smile, 'then I guess you already know.'

The visitors who truly touched me, though, the ones I remember clearly, were the young parents from Texas and their six-year-old daughter. As soon as they entered the library, it was clear this was a special trip for her. Was she sick? Was she dealing with a trauma? I don't know why, but I had the feeling the parents offered her one wish, and this was it. The girl wanted to meet Dewey. And, I noticed, she had brought a present.

'It's a toy mouse,' her father told me. He was smiling, but I could tell he was intensely worried. This was no ordinary spur-of-the-moment visit.

As I smiled back at him, only one thought was going through my mind: 'I hope that toy mouse has catnip in it.' Dewey would regularly go through periods where he wanted nothing to do with any toy that didn't contain catnip. Unfortunately this was one of those times.

All I said was, 'I'll go get Dewey.'

Dewey was asleep in his new fake fur-lined bed, which we kept outside my office door in front of a heating unit. As I woke him up I tried a little mental telepathy: 'Please, Dewey, please. This one's important.' He was so tired, he barely opened his eyes.

The little girl was hesitant at first, as many children are, so the mother petted Dewey first. Dewey lay there like a sack of potatoes. The girl eventually reached out to pet him, and Dewey woke up enough to lean into her hand. The father sat down and put both Dewey and the girl on his lap. Dewey immediately snuggled up against her.

They sat like that for a minute or two. Finally the girl showed him the present she had brought, with its carefully tied ribbon and bow. Dewey perked up, but I could tell he was still tired. He would have preferred to snooze in the girl's lap all morning. 'Come on, Dewey,' I thought. 'Snap out of it.' The girl unwrapped the gift, and sure enough, it was a plain toy mouse, no catnip in sight. My heart sank. This was going to be a disaster.

The girl dangled the mouse in front of Dewey's sleepy eyes to get his attention. Then she delicately tossed it a few feet away. As soon as it hit the ground, Dewey jumped on it. He chased that toy; he threw it in the air; he batted it with his paws. The girl giggled with delight. Dewey never played with it again, but while that little girl was here, he loved that little mouse. He gave that mouse every ounce of energy he had. And the little girl beamed. She just beamed. She had come hundreds of miles to see a cat, and she was not disappointed. Why did I ever worry about Dewey? He always came through.

DEWEY'S JOB DESCRIPTION

Written in response to the question,
'So what is Dewey's job?'
which was often asked after people
found out Dewey received a
15 percent library employee
discount from Dr. Esterly.

1. Reducing stress for all humans who pay
   attention to him.

2. Sitting by the front door every morning
   at nine to greet the public as they enter
   the library.

3. Sampling all boxes that enter the
   library for security problems and
   comfort level.

4. Attending all meetings in the Round
   Room as official library ambassador.

5. Providing comic relief for staff and
   visitors.

6. Climbing in book bags and briefcases while patrons are studying or trying to retrieve needed papers.

7. Generating free national and worldwide publicity for Spencer Public Library. (This entails sitting still for photographs, smiling for the camera, and generally being cute.)

8. Working toward status as world's most finicky cat by refusing all but the most expensive, delectable foods.

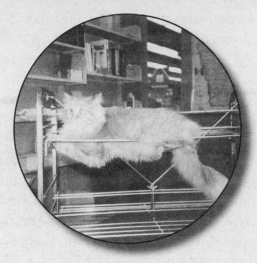

21

What Makes Us Special?

I 'll always remember the former city manager. Every time he saw me, he said with a smile, 'Are you girls at the library still mooning over that cat?' Maybe he was trying to be funny, but I couldn't help but feel offended. *Girls!* That word might be a term of endearment, but I got the feeling he was putting me in my place, that he was speaking for a large block of community leaders who couldn't even conceive of making a fuss over things like books, libraries, and cats. That was *girl* stuff.

Did the town even need a cat anymore? It was the twenty-first century, after all, and Spencer was thriving. In the late 1990s, the YMCA completed a $2 million renovation. The Spencer Regional Hospital expanded twice. Thanks to $170,000 in donations and 250 volunteers, the modest new playground planned for East Lynch Park turned into a 30,000-square-foot megaplayground called the Miracle on South Fourth Street. Why not just take the next step and attract . . . a casino?

When Iowa decided to issue a few casino licenses in 2003, some community leaders sensed an opportunity to catapult Spencer into the biggest little small town in America. They courted developers, even picked out a location along the river on the southwest edge of town, and drew up plans. But for many of us, the casino in 2003 looked like the slaughterhouse in 1993 – a chance to put on economic muscle, but at a high cost. Sure, the casino would generate good jobs and, according to estimates, more than a million dollars in mandatory charitable contributions a year, but would we ever be the same town again? Would we lose our identity and become, in our own eyes and everyone else's around, the casino town? The debate went back and forth, but in the end the casino met the same fate as the Montfort plant: the community voted it down. The casino was authorized in Palo Alto County, the county east of us, and built in Emmetsburg, only twenty-five miles away.

Maybe when we voted down the casino we once again turned our backs on the future. Maybe we were selling out our history as a progressive town. Maybe we were being naïve. But in Spencer we believe in building on what we have.

We have the Clay County Fair, one of the best county fairs in the United States and a tradition for almost a hundred years. Clay County has fewer than 20,000 residents, but the fair attracts more than 300,000 people for nine days of rides, concerts, food, and fun. We have a full-size track for races and tractor pulls, a separate ring for horses, and long metal barns for everything from chickens to llamas. There are hay wagons to take you from the parking lot (a grass field) to the front gate. We've even installed a sky bucket system to carry people from one end of the fair to the other. There's a year-round sign about ten miles south of Spencer, on the main road (and only road if you're driving more than a few miles), that counts down the weeks to the fair. It's painted on a brick building built on the highest hill in the area.

We have Grand Avenue, a historic treasure, rebuilt in 1931 and revived in 1987. In the late 1990s, our city planner, Kirby Schmidt, spent two years researching our downtown strip. Kirby was one of the native sons who almost left Spencer during the crisis of the 1980s. His brother left for the East Coast, his sister for the West Coast. Kirby sat down at the kitchen table with his young family, and they decided to stick it out. The economy turned; Kirby got a job with the city. A few years later, I gave him the key to the library, and he started coming in at six every morning to search through microfiche files, old newspapers, and local histories. Dewey mostly slept through these early visits; in the morning, he only had eyes for me.

In 1999, Grand Avenue between Third Street and Eighth Street was placed on the National Register of Historic Places. The area was cited as a remarkable example of Prairie Deco and one of the few surviving comprehensive models of Depression-era urban planning. It usually took two or three applications to make the Registry, but thanks to Kirby Schmidt, Grand Avenue made it by unanimous vote on the first application. Around the same time, Kirby's sister moved her family back to Spencer from Seattle. She wanted to raise her kids the old-fashioned way: in Iowa.

That's another of Spencer's unique and valuable assets: its people. We are good, solid, hardworking midwesterners. We are proud but humble. We don't brag. We believe your worth is measured by the respect of your neighbors, and there is no place we'd rather be than with those neighbors right here in Spencer, Iowa. We are woven not just into this land, which our families have worked for generations, but to one another. And a bright shining thread, popping up in a hundred places in that tapestry, is Dewey.

In our society, people believe you have to *do* something to be recognized, by which we mean something 'in your face,' and preferably caught on camera. We expect a famous town to survive a tsunami and a forest fire or produce a president or cover up some horrible crime. We expect a famous cat to save a child from a burning building, find his way home after being left behind on the other side of the country, or meow 'The Star-Spangled Banner.' And that cat better be not just heroic and talented, but media savvy, attractive, and have a good press agent, too, or he's never going to make it onto the *Today* show.

Dewey wasn't like that. He didn't perform spectacular feats. There was nobody pushing him to success. We didn't want him to be anything more than the beloved library cat of Spencer, Iowa. And that's all he wanted, too. He ran away only once, and he went only two blocks, and even that was too far.

Dewey wasn't special because he *did* something extraordinary but because he *was* extraordinary. He was like one of those seemingly ordinary people who, once you get to know them, stand out from the crowd. They are the ones who never miss a day of work, who never complain, who never ask for more than their share. They are those rare librarians, car salesmen, and waitresses who provide excellent service on principle, who go beyond the job because they have a passion for the job. They know what they are meant to do in life, and they do it exceptionally well. Some win awards; some make a lot of money; most are taken for granted. The store clerks. The bank tellers. The auto mechanics. The mothers. The world tends to recognize the unique and the loud, the rich and the self-serving, not those who do ordinary things extraordinarily well. Dewey came from humble beginnings (an Iowa alley); he survived tragedy (a freezing drop box); he found his place (a small-town library). Maybe that's the answer. He found his place. His passion, his purpose, was to make that place, no matter how small and out of the way it may have seemed, a better place for everyone.

I don't want to take anything away from the cat who falls out of the Winnebago, then spends five months trudging home through snowdrifts and scorching heat. That cat is an inspiration: never give up, always remember the importance of home. In his quiet way, Dewey taught those lessons, too. He never gave up during his long night in the box, and he was devoted to the library that became his home. Dewey didn't do one heroic thing; he did something heroic every day. He spent his time changing lives right here in Spencer, Iowa, one lap at a time.

You've no doubt noticed the strings on a fresh ear of corn. Those are the silks. Each one is connected to a particular spot on the ear. The spot grows a kernel only if that particular string is fertilized by pollen. The ear is made piece by piece, one kernel at a time. For an ear of corn to be whole, every silk must be fertilized. That's the way Dewey operated. He won hearts day by day, one person at a time. He never left anyone out or took anyone for granted. If you were receptive, he was there for you. If you weren't receptive, he worked to bring you around. Surely you know Wilbur, the pig in *Charlotte's Web*. Dewey had that personality: enthusiastic, honest, charming, radiant, humble (for a cat), and above all, a friend to anyone and everyone. It wasn't just beauty. It wasn't just a great story. Dewey had charisma, like Elvis or any of the other people who will live in our minds forever. There are dozens of library cats in the United States, but none come close to accomplishing what Dewey accomplished. He wasn't just another cat for people to pet and smile about. Every regular user of the library, *every single one*, felt they had a unique relationship with Dewey. He made everyone feel special.

Sharon often brought her daughter Emmy, who had Down syndrome, to see Dewey, especially on Sunday when it was her turn to feed him. Every Saturday night Emmy asked her, 'Is tomorrow a Dewey day?' The first thing Emmy did every 'Dewey day' was search for Dewey. When he was younger, he would usually be waiting by the door, but as he aged Emmy often found him lying in the sun by a window. She would pick him up and bring him to Mommy so they could pet him together. 'Hi, Dewey. I love you,' Emmy would say in a soft, kind voice, the way her own mother talked to her. For Emmy, that was the voice of love. Sharon was always afraid Emmy would pet him too hard, but Emmy and Dewey were friends, and she understood him as well as any of us. She was always wonderfully gentle.

Yvonne Berry, a single woman in her late thirties, came to the library three or four times a week. Every time, Dewey sought her out and spent fifteen minutes on her lap. Then he tried to coax her to open the bathroom door so he could play with the water. It was their ritual. But on the day Yvonne had to put her own cat to sleep, Dewey sat with her for more than two hours. He didn't know what had happened, but he knew something was wrong. Years later, when she told me that story, I could tell it was still important to her.

The century was turning, changing over, and Dewey was mellowing. He spent more time in his cat bed, and strenuous play was replaced by quiet book cart rides with Joy. Instead of jumping onto the cart, he would meow for Joy to pick him up so he could ride at the front of the cart like the captain of a ship. He stopped jumping to the ceiling lights, more out of boredom, I believe, than physical necessity. He couldn't abide rough handling, but he loved a gentle touch, like that of the homeless man who became one of his best friends. It is difficult to be invisible in a town like Spencer, but this man came close. He simply appeared at the library every day, unshaven, uncombed, and unwashed. He never said a word to anyone. He never looked at anyone. He wanted only Dewey. He would pick Dewey up and drape him over his shoulder; Dewey would lie there, purring, for twenty minutes while the man unburdened himself of secrets.

When Dewey gave up walking the top of the wall shelves, Kay took his old cat bed and put it on top of her desk hutch. Dewey would snuggle up in that bed and watch Kay work. Kay was attentive to Dewey's needs, changing his food, brushing his tangles, giving him Vaseline for fur balls, helping me with his bath. She wasn't as patient or gentle as I was, but even her roughest handling ended with a tender moment and a soft chuck on the head. One day not too long after Kay set up the new arrangement, Dewey jumped up to the bed and the shelf collapsed. The cat flew one way, four legs flailing. Notepads and paper clips flew the other. Before the last paper clip had hit the floor, Dewey was back to survey the damage.

'Not scared of too much in this library, are you?' Kay joked, a smile that I could tell reached all the way down to her heart curling the corners of her mouth.

Only the brush and the bath, Dewey would have said if he was being honest. The older Dewey got, the more he hated being groomed.

He also didn't have as much patience for preschool children, who tended to poke and pull at him. He was stiffening up, and he could no longer tolerate the small knocks and bruises. He never lashed out at children, and he rarely ran from them. He simply began to scoot away and hide when certain children came looking for him, avoiding a situation before it began.

Babies were a different story. One day I watched Dewey plop himself down a few feet from an infant girl who was on the floor in a baby carrier. I had often seen Dewey interact with infants, so I wasn't apprehensive. But babies are delicate, and new moms even more so. Especially this one. Dewey just sat with a bored expression, looking off into the distance as if to say, *Just happened to be walking by.* Then, when he thought I wasn't looking, he squirmed an inch closer. *Just adjusting my position,* his body language said, *nothing to see here.* A minute later, he did it again. Then again. Slowly, inch by inch, he crept closer, until finally he was pressed right up against the carrier. He popped his head over the edge, as if to confirm the child was inside, then settled down with his head on his paws. The infant reached her little hand over the edge and snatched his ear. Dewey adjusted his head so she could get a better grip. She laughed, kicking her legs and squeezing his ear. Dewey sat quietly, a contented look on his face.

We hired a new assistant children's librarian, Donna Stanford, in 2002. Donna had been around the world as a Peace Corps recruiter, and she had recently returned to northwest Iowa to care for her mother, who was suffering from Alzheimer's. Donna was quiet and conscientious, which I thought at first was the reason Dewey spent a few hours every day with her over in the children's section. It took me a long time to realize that Donna didn't know anyone in town besides her mother, and that even a place like Spencer – or maybe especially a close-knit place like Spencer – could seem cold and intimidating to an outsider. The only local resident who reached out to Donna was Dewey, who would ride on her shoulder while she rolled around in her office chair shelving books. When he tired of that, he would climb down onto her lap so Donna could pet him. Sometimes she read him children's books. I caught them by surprise one day, Dewey resting with his eyes closed, Donna deep in thought. I could tell she was startled.

'Don't worry,' I said. 'It is part of your job description to hold the kitty.'

Then there was Jodi's boyfriend, Scott. Poor Scott was thrown right into the fire on his first trip to Spencer: my parents' fiftieth wedding anniversary. And this wasn't just a family party. The event was held at the Spencer Convention Center, which had a seating capacity of 450 people. Even the convention center couldn't contain the crowd. When the Jipson children descended on the stage to perform – in this case 'You Are My Sunshine' with family-themed lyrics and Vince Gill's 'Look at Us,' complete with my brother Doug's flat, off-key warbling – there were still more than a hundred people lined up outside, waiting to congratulate Mom and Dad. All their lives they had treated the whole world as their family; now the world had come to honor them.

As soon as she left home, my relationship with Jodi improved dramatically. We were great friends, we realized, and terrible roommates. But while we laughed about the present, we still didn't talk about the past. Maybe mothers and daughters never do. That didn't mean I couldn't try.

'I know we've had some hard times, Jodi.'

'What are you talking about, Mom?'

Where should I start? My health. My absences. Her messy room. Brandy. 'In Mankato. Remember? We would walk by a store and you'd say "I really want that shirt, Mommy, but I know we don't have any money, so that's okay." You didn't want it, you needed it, but you never wanted me to feel bad.' I sighed. 'You were only five years old.'

'Oh, Mom, that's just life.'

And right then I realized that she was right. The good, the bad, that's just life. Let it go. There's no need to fret about the past. The question is: who are you going to share it with tomorrow?

That night, after the party, Jodi and I took Scott to the library to meet Dewey. That's when I knew this relationship was serious; Jodi had never introduced Dewey to one of her boyfriends before, and none of her other boyfriends, as far as I knew, had ever been interested in meeting him. Dewey was, of course, overjoyed to see Jodi. She was forever his love. Scott gave the two of them time together, then gently picked Dewey up and petted him. Not on the stomach, which Dewey hated, but along the back. He walked him around the empty library in the Dewey Carry. He pulled out his camera and took a snapshot for his mother. She had heard the Dewey stories, and she was a big fan. My heart warmed to see the two of them together. Scott was so loving and tender. And how could I not fall for a guy thoughtful enough to take a photograph for his mom?

It never occurred to me there was anything unusual about taking a grown woman's boyfriend to a library to meet her mother's cat. Dewey was part of the family; his opinion mattered. How could anyone seriously consider being a part of this family without knowing him? And I trusted Dewey to sniff out a rat; he was my sentry, always protecting the ones he loved. Seeing Scott with Dewey, and Dewey with Scott, told me everything I needed to know.

It also never crossed my mind, at this point, to think of Dewey as the library's cat. Dewey was my cat. I was the person he came to for love. I was the person he came to for comfort. And I went to him for love and comfort, too. He wasn't a substitute husband or a substitute child. I wasn't lonely; I had plenty of friends. I wasn't unfulfilled; I loved my job. I wasn't looking for someone special. It wasn't even that I saw him every day. We lived apart. We could spend whole days in the library together and hardly see each other. But even when I didn't see him, I knew he was there. We had chosen, I realized, to share our lives, not just tomorrow, but forever.

Dewey was more special to me than any animal I had ever known. He was more special to me than I ever believed an animal could be. However, that didn't change a fundamental truth. He was my cat, but he belonged in the library. His place was with the public. Dewey was happy at my house for a day or two, but as soon as we got in the car and headed downtown to the library, he put his front feet on the dashboard and stared excitedly out the window. I had to take the turns slowly, or he'd slide right off. When he smelled

Sister's Café, Dewey knew we were a few blocks away. That's when he got really excited. He'd move to the armrest and put his paws on the side window, practically willing the door to open. *We're here! We're here!* He'd look over his shoulder and practically yell it to me when we entered the alley. As soon as the door opened, he jumped into my arms and I carried him across the threshold. And then . . . bliss.

There was nothing Dewey loved more than being home.

22

Dewey Goes to Japan

W e received the e-mail from Japan in early 2003. Actually, the e-mail came from Washington, D.C., on behalf of people in Tokyo. Tomoko Kawasumi represented Japanese Public Television, which wanted to film Dewey. The company was making a documentary to introduce some new high-definition technology, and they wanted as wide an audience as possible. They decided first on a documentary about animals, then narrowed the focus to cats. They discovered Dewey through a feature in the Japanese magazine *Nekobiyori*. Would we mind if a film crew came to Spencer for a day?

That's funny, we had no idea Dewey had appeared in a Japanese magazine.

A few months later, in May, six people from Tokyo arrived at the Spencer Public Library. They had flown to Des Moines, rented a van, and driven to Spencer. Iowa in May is beautiful. The corn is just below eye level, three or four feet tall, so you can see the fields spreading into the distance. Of course, it's two hundred miles from Des Moines to Spencer, and that's all you can see, mile after mile. What were six people from Tokyo thinking after three and a half hours of looking at Iowa corn? We'd have to ask them, because they were probably the only people from Tokyo ever to make that drive.

The crew had one day to film, so they asked me to arrive at the library before seven. It was a miserably rainy morning. The interpreter, the only woman in the group, asked me to open the first set of doors so they could set up their cameras in the lobby. As they were carting equipment, around the corner came Dewey. He was half asleep, stretching his back legs as cats often do when they first wake up. When he saw me, he trotted over and gave me a wave. *Oh, it's you. What are you doing here so early? I wasn't expecting you for twenty minutes.* You could have set your watch by that cat.

Once the crew set up the cameras, the interpreter said, 'We'd like him to wave again.'

Oh, brother. I tried to explain, as best I could, that Dewey waved only once, when he saw me first thing in the morning. The director, Mr. Hoshi, wouldn't hear of it. He was used not only to giving orders but to having them obeyed. He was definitely the man in charge. And right now, he wanted that wave.

So I went back to my car and approached the library again, pretending I hadn't been in that morning. Dewey just stared at me.

What? You were just here five minutes ago.

I entered the library, turned on the lights, turned off the lights, went back to the car, waited five minutes, and approached the library again. Mr. Hoshi thought this might fool Dewey into thinking it was the next day.

It didn't.

We tried for an hour to get footage of Dewey waving. Finally I said, 'Look, the poor cat has been sitting there this whole time waiting for his food. I have to feed him.' Mr. Hoshi agreed. I scooped Dewey up and rushed to the litter box. The last thing I wanted the Japanese to get on film was flying poop. Dewey relieved himself, then ate a leisurely breakfast. By the time he was finished, the camera crew was set up inside. They had come halfway around the world, and they never got their wave.

But they got everything else. Dewey was almost fifteen years old and he was slowing down, but he hadn't lost his enthusiasm for strangers. Especially strangers with cameras. He approached each member of the crew and greeted him with a rub on the leg. They were petting him, horsing around, and one cameraman lay down on the floor for a Dewey-eye view. The interpreter politely asked me to put Dewey on a bookshelf. He sat there and let them film. He jumped from shelf to shelf. Then she said, 'Have him walk down the shelf between the books and jump off the end.'

I thought, 'Wait a second. He's a cat, not a trained animal in the circus, and that's a pretty specific request. I hope you didn't come all this way expecting a show because there's no way he's going to walk that shelf, slalom between the display books, and jump off at command.'

I trudged down to the far end of the shelf and called, 'Come here, Dewey. Come here.' Dewey walked down the shelf, slalomed between the books, and jumped down to my feet.

For five hours Mr. Hoshi gave orders and Dewey complied. He sat on a computer. He sat on a table. He sat on the floor with his feet crossed and stared into the camera. He rode on his favorite book cart with his feet hanging down through the openings in the metal grill, completely relaxed. No time to dally; move, move, move. A three-year-old girl and her mother agreed to appear in the film, so I put Dewey on the glider chair with them. The girl was nervous, grabbing and pulling at Dewey. Dewey didn't mind. He sat through the whole five-minute ordeal and never forgot to stare sweetly at the camera.

I had been telling the interpreter all morning that people came from all over the United States to visit

Dewey, but I don't think Mr. Hoshi believed me. Then, just after lunch, in walked a family from New Hampshire. Talk about timing! The family was at a wedding in Des Moines and decided to rent a car and drive up to see Dewey. Need I remind you that's a three-and-a-half-hour drive?

Mr. Hoshi was all over the visitors. He interviewed them extensively. He took footage of them shooting their own footage of Dewey with their camcorder (probably manufactured in Japan). I taught the girl, who was five or six, the Dewey Carry, and how to gently rock back and forth until he put his head down on her back and closed his eyes. The family stayed an hour; the Japanese crew left soon after. As soon as they were gone, Dewey fell asleep and was out the rest of the day.

We received two copies of the DVD. After sixteen years, I was reluctant to talk about Dewey too much, but this seemed special. I called the newspaper. The electronics store on the corner loaned us a giant projection television, and we packed the library. By this time, Dewey had been on the radio in Canada and New Zealand. He had appeared in newspapers and magazines in dozens of countries. His photograph had been all over the world. But this was different. This was worldwide television!

I had sneaked a peak at the video, so I was a little nervous. The documentary turned out to be an alphabetic trip through the world of cats. There were twenty-six featured cats, one for each letter of the alphabet. Yes, our alphabet, even though the documentary was in Japanese.

I told the audience, 'There are a lot of other cats in this documentary. Dewey is near the end, and the whole thing is in Japanese, so let's take a vote. Should we fast-forward to Dewey's part or watch the whole thing?'

'Watch the whole thing! Watch the whole thing!'

Ten minutes late the crowd was shouting, 'Fast-forward! Fast-forward!' Let's just say it was extremely boring to watch jump cuts of cats and interviews in Japanese. We stopped for especially cute cats, or every time there was an American on screen – we stopped twice for that reason, but one of the women turned out to be British – but most of the footage was of Japanese people and their pets.

When we hit the letter *W*, a cry went up around the room, no doubt waking the snoozers. There was our Dewey, along with the words *Working Cat* in English and Japanese. There I was walking up to the library in the rain, while the announcer said something in Japanese. We understood only three words: 'America, Iowa-shun, Spencer.' Another loud cheer. A few seconds later we heard: 'Dewey a-Deedamore Booksa.'

And there was Dewey, sitting at the front door (I have to admit, a wave would have been nice), followed by Dewey sitting on a bookshelf, Dewey walking through two bookshelves, Dewey sitting, and sitting, and sitting and being petted by a little boy under a table and . . . sitting. One and a half minutes, and it was over. No little girl with Dewey on her lap. No riding the shoulder. No book cart. No family from New Hampshire. They didn't even use the shot of Dewey walking on top of the bookshelf, slaloming between the books, and jumping off the end. They came halfway around the world for a minute and a half of sitting.

Silence. Stunned silence.

And then a huge burst of cheering. Our Dewey was an international star. Here was the proof. So what if we didn't have a clue what the announcer was saying? So what if Dewey's portion lasted barely longer than a typical commercial break? There was our library. There was our librarian. There was our Dewey. And the announcer definitely said, 'America, Iowa-shun, Spencer.'

The town of Spencer has never forgotten that Japanese documentary. Maybe its contents. We have two copies for checkout in the library, but nobody ever watches them. *Puss in Books* is much more popular. But the fact that a film crew came from Tokyo to Spencer, that's something we'll never forget. The local radio station and the newspaper both ran long features, and for months people came into the library to talk about it.

'What was the crew like?'

'What did they do?'

'Where did they go while in town?'

'What else did they film?'

'Can you believe it?'

'Can you believe it?'

'Can you believe it?'

Japanese television put Dewey over the top. Even today, when locals talk about Dewey, the conversation always comes around to, 'And those Japanese people came here, to Spencer, to film him.' What more needs to be said?

Spencer residents aren't the only ones who remember that documentary. After it aired, we received several letters from Japan and forty requests for Dewey postcards. Our library Web site tallies the origin of visitors, and every month since the documentary aired in the summer of 2004 Japan has been the second most popular country of origin, after the United States – more than 150,000 visitors in three years. Somehow, I don't think they're interested in checking out books.

But the Japanese invasion wasn't the only special thing that happened during the summer of 2003, at least for me. The previous year, Scott had proposed to Jodi on Christmas Eve at my parents' house. She asked me to take charge of the flowers and decorations, since both were hobbies of mine.

But there was something nagging at me. My sister, Val, was Jodi's maid of honor, and I knew the two of them were discussing dresses. I didn't have a chance to choose my own wedding dress. A girl in Hartley had called off her wedding at the last minute, and Mom bought her dress for me. I wanted more than anything to help Jodi pick her wedding dress. I wanted the dress to be special. I wanted to be a part of it. I called Jodi and said, 'I've dreamed all my life of helping you pick out your wedding dress. Val has two daughters of her own. She'll have her chance.'

'I would love to do this with you, Mom.'

My heart leaped into my throat. I could tell by the quiver in Jodi's voice that she felt it, too. We are both sentimental fools.

But I'm also practical. 'You narrow down the choices,' I told her. 'When you find half a dozen you like, I'll drive there to help you make the final decision.' Jodi could never make up her mind about clothes. She kept most of her garments in their original boxes, because she was always returning them. Jodi lived more than three hours away in Omaha, Nebraska, and I didn't want to kill myself making that drive every weekend for the next six months.

Jodi shopped for dresses with her friends. Weeks later I drove to Omaha to help her make the final decision. We couldn't decide. Then we spotted one she'd never tried on. As soon as we saw her in the dress, we knew. Jodi and I stood in the dressing room together and cried.

We went shopping together a few months later, and she chose a beautiful dress for me. Then Jodi called me and said, 'I just bought a dress for Grandma.'

'That's funny,' I told her. 'I was in Des Moines on library business, and I bought her one, too.' When we got together, we realized we had bought Mom the same dress on the same day at the same time. We really laughed about that one.

The wedding took place in July at St. Joseph Catholic Church in Milford, Iowa. Jodi planned the wedding from Omaha; I did the legwork. My old friends from Mankato, Trudy, Barb, Faith, and Idelle, came down a few days before the ceremony to help me set up. Jodi and I were perfectionists; we didn't want a flower out of place. Trudy and Barb were nervous wrecks when we decorated Mom and Dad's garage for the reception, but they did a beautiful job. When they finished, it didn't even resemble a garage. The next day we decorated the church, then the restaurant for the rehearsal dinner.

There were thirty-seven guests at the wedding, just family members and close friends. My friends didn't attend the ceremony; they were in a back room heating butterflies. The butterflies were supposed to be kept on ice, in suspended animation, then warmed up and 'awoken' fifteen minutes before being called upon to fly. Faith called herself the BBBBB – the Beautiful Big-Boobed Butterfly Babysitter – but she took her job quite seriously. She was so nervous about the butterflies, the night before the wedding she took them to Trudy's house in Worthington, Minnesota, an hour away, and kept them beside her bed.

When the guests came out of the wedding, Scott's parents handed each of them an envelope. My brother Mike, who was standing next to the bride, immediately started squeezing. Jodi gave him a look.

'What?' Mike said. 'Is it alive?'

'Well, it *was*.'

I read the legend of the butterflies, which have no voices. When released, they rise to heaven and whisper our wishes to God.

When the guests opened their envelopes, butterflies of all sizes and colors flew up into a beautiful clear blue sky, a whisper away from God. Most of them disappeared on the wind. Three settled back down on Jodi's dress. One stayed on her bridal bouquet for more than an hour.

After wedding photos, the guests piled into a bus. While my friends cleaned up, the rest of us rode to West Okoboji for a lake tour on the *Queen II*, the area's famous sightseeing boat. Afterward Jodi and Scott decided to ride the Arnold Park Ferris wheel, the same one that had glistened in the night when Mom and Dad were falling in love to the sound of Tommy Dorsey at the Roof Garden so many decades before. As the rest of us watched, the Ferris wheel took Jodi and Scott, along with the ring bearer and the flower girl, up, up, up into that clear blue sky, like butterflies slipping out of their envelopes and taking flight.

The letter Jodi sent after the honeymoon said it all: 'Thank you, Mom. It was the perfect wedding.' No eight words could ever make me happier.

If only life were that easy. If only Dewey, Jodi, and the whole Jipson family could be frozen right there, in the summer of 2003. But even as that Ferris wheel rose, even as Dewey became a star in Japan, there was a stain on the picture. Only a few months before, Mom had been diagnosed with leukemia, the latest in a long line of illnesses to try to strike her down. They say cancer, like luck, runs in a family. Unfortunately, cancer runs deep in the Jipson line.

23

Memories of Mom

My brother Steven was diagnosed with stage four non-Hodgkin's lymphoma, the most advanced form of a lethal cancer, in 1976. The doctors gave him two months to live. He was nineteen years old.

Steven dealt with his cancer with more dignity than anybody I have ever known. He battled it, but not desperately. He lived his life, too. He never lost his sense of self. But the cancer was in his chest, and they couldn't beat it. They knocked it down, but it came back. The treatment was painful, and it ate through Steven's kidneys. My brother Mike, Steven's best friend, offered to give him one of his kidneys, but Steven told him, 'Don't bother. I'll just ruin that one, too.'

As I struggled with a divorce, welfare, and college, Steven struggled with cancer. By 1979, he had lived longer than anyone in Iowa had ever lived with stage four non-Hodgkin's lymphoma. The doctors had given him so much chemotherapy, he had no blood left in his extremities. There was no hope left in chemo, so Steven enrolled in an experimental treatment center in Houston. He was scheduled to start in January, and before the trip he wanted a full-scale, no-holds-barred Jipson Christmas. Steven wanted the clam chowder Dad always made on Christmas Eve. He wanted me to make his favorite caramel popcorn. He sat under a blanket and smiled along as we played our homemade instruments in the Jipson Family Band. It was eighteen below zero on Christmas Eve; Steven couldn't even stand, he was so weak, but he insisted we all go to Midnight Mass. On his last night at Mom and Dad's house, he made me drive him to Aunt Marlene's house at two in the morning to say good-bye. Afterward, he wanted me to stay up with him and watch *Brian's Song*, a movie about a football player with cancer.

'No thanks, Stevie. I've already seen it.'

But he insisted, so I stayed up with him. He fell asleep in the first five minutes.

A week later, on January 6, Steven woke his wife at 5:00 a.m. and asked her to help him down the stairs to the sofa. When she came back down a few hours later, she couldn't wake him. We found out later he hadn't been enrolled in an experimental treatment program in Houston. The day before Thanksgiving, the doctors had told him there were no more treatment options left. He hadn't told anyone because he wanted one last Jipson family Christmas, free from crying and pity, before he died.

My parents took Steven's death hard. Death can drive two people apart, but it drove Mom and Dad together. They cried together. They talked together. They leaned on each other. My father converted to Catholicism, Mom's religion, and started attending church regularly for the first time in his adult life.

And they adopted a cat.

Three weeks after Steven's death, Dad bought Mom a blue Persian and named him Max. Those were terrible days for them, just terrible, but Max was a sainted cat, full of personality but not wild. He would sleep in the bathroom sink; with the exception of snuggling up against Mom's side, that sink was his favorite place in the house. If ever a cat changed a couple, it was Max. He raised my parents' spirits. He made them laugh. He kept them company in their empty home. The children loved Max for his personality, but we loved him more for taking care of Mom and Dad.

My older brother David, my dear friend and inspiration, was also deeply affected by Steven's death. David had dropped out of college six weeks before graduation and after a few false starts ended up in Mason City, Iowa, about a hundred miles east of Spencer. When I think of David, though, I think of Mankato, Minnesota. The two of us were so close in Mankato. We had a wonderful time together, simply wonderful. But one night, shortly before he dropped out of college and moved away, he knocked on my door at one in the morning. It was ten below zero, and he had walked ten miles.

He said, 'There's something wrong with me, Vicki. In my head. I think I'm having a breakdown. But you can't tell Mom and Dad. Promise me you'll never tell Mom and Dad.'

I was nineteen years old, young and stupid. I promised. I never told anyone about that night, but I know now that mental illness often strikes young men, especially bright and talented young men in their early twenties like David. I know David was ill. He was as ill as Steven had been, but it wasn't as obvious. Slowly, his condition pulled his life downward. Within a few years, he was a different person. He couldn't hold a job. He couldn't laugh, even with me. He started taking drugs, downers mostly, to combat depression. He fathered a child out of wedlock. He called me every few months, and we talked for hours, but over the years I heard from him less and less.

When Steven died in January 1980, David coped with drugs. He said he couldn't function without them. His daughter, Mackenzie, was four, and her mother cut David off from contact with her until he kicked his habit. Eight months after Steven died, David phoned me in the middle of the night to tell me he had lost his daughter.

'You haven't lost Mackenzie,' I told him. 'If you're straight, you can visit her. If you're high, you can't. It's that simple.'

He couldn't see it. We talked about a million things that night, but nothing I suggested was possible. He had a blank wall in front of him. He couldn't see any future at all. I was scared to death, but he swore he wouldn't do anything until we talked again. He loved his daughter, he assured me, and he would never leave her. But sometime later that night or early the next morning, my brother David, my childhood buddy, picked up a shotgun and pulled the trigger.

My friend Trudy drove me to Hartley at two in the morning. I could barely breathe; there was no way I could drive. My parents were no better. None of us wanted to face David's death, especially so soon after Steven's, but it was there whether we wanted it or not. A few days after the funeral, David's landlord started calling my parents' house and pestering them. He was screaming at us to come get David's things, to clean out the apartment, so he could rent it again. It was another reminder that David didn't live in the best area or associate with the kindest people.

We drove to Mason City in two vehicles. Dad, my brothers Mike and Doug, and two of David's old friends drove ahead in the car. My mother, Val, and I followed in a truck. When we arrived, the men were standing at the curb.

'You're not going in there,' Dad said. 'Wait here. We'll bring everything out.'

We didn't know it until Dad opened the door, but nobody had touched the apartment since David's death. The mess from what David had done, it was everywhere. Dad, Mike, and Doug had to wipe everything down before bringing it out to pack in the truck. I can still see the stains. David's possessions were meager, to say the least, but it took all day to move them. Dad, Mike, and Doug didn't say a word, and they've never spoken about that day since. When I told him I was writing this book, Dad asked me not to mention David. It wasn't shame or secrecy. There were tears in his eyes. Even after all this time, it's too painful for him to talk about. But talk we must.

Two weeks after David's death, it was time to have Max fixed. The vet gave him the anesthetic and left for ten minutes to give it time to work. Unfortunately he didn't remove the water dish from his cage. The dish held only half an inch of water, but Max fell in and drowned.

I happened to be there when the veterinarian came to the house. He knew my family. He knew what my parents were going through. Now he had to tell them he had killed their cat. We all stared at him for half a minute, speechless. 'I loved that cat with a passion,' Dad finally said, calmly but firmly. 'You son of a bitch.' Then he turned and walked upstairs. He couldn't even speak to the guy. He couldn't look at him. Dad still feels bad about his outburst, but Max's death was too much. It was simply too much.

When Mom was diagnosed with leukemia in the spring of 2003, she and Dad adopted a kitten. Mom hadn't owned a Persian in twenty years, since the death of Max. But instead of adopting a Persian as they intended, they came back with a Himalayan, a cross between a Persian and a Siamese. He was a gray beauty with silky blue eyes, the spitting image of Max right down to the outgoing and loving personality. They named him Max II.

Max II was the first admission Mom was going to die. Not from Dad. My mother was so strong, Dad believed she could survive anything. The admission came from Mom. She knew this illness was the one to beat her, and she didn't want Dad to be alone.

Mom was a force of nature. I suspect she started out running from life, from her alcoholic father and the long hours she worked in the family restaurant, even as a five-year-old child. When my grandmother divorced, she and Mom took jobs in a women's clothing store. That was her life, her future, until she met Dad.

After she met Verlyn Jipson, Marie Mayou turned around and spent every moment running toward life. My mother and father loved each other deeply. Their love was so great it can't be contained in this or any book. They loved their children. They loved to sing

and dance. They loved their friends, their town, their
lives. They were great ones for celebrations. They
would throw a party for every accomplishment and
milestone. Mom would get up early to do the cooking,
and she'd stay up until three in the morning when
everyone finally left. At six the next morning, she'd
start cleaning. By eight, the house was immaculate.
Mom's house was always immaculate.

Mom was diagnosed with breast cancer in the
early 1970s. The doctors gave her no chance to live,
but she beat it. She beat it not once but five times,
twice in one breast and three times in the other. She
beat it with a whole lot of strength and a whole lot of
faith. My friend Bonnie and I used to call Mom 'the
number two Catholic in the world.' When Jodi was
eight, she and I were riding our bikes in Hartley when
we happened to pass the small building that used to
house St. Joseph Catholic Church. Mom had been on
the planning committee for the new building, and the
two trees in front were planted in memory of Steven
and David. Jodi looked at the old wooden building
and said, 'Mom, was Grandma as crazy about church
when you were growing up as she is now?'

'Yes,' I told her, 'she sure was.'

Mom's faith came from the church, but her
strength came from inside. She simply wouldn't give
in to anything. Not pain, not tiredness, not sorrow.
When Mom fought her third bout with breast cancer,
her stepmother, Lucille, drove her every day to
Sioux City, four hours round-trip, for eight weeks.

Radiation treatment in those days was much worse than it is today. They basically blasted you until your body couldn't take any more. Mom was burned to a crisp. She had an open wound the size of a large pancake under her arm, and it was so chewed up Dad would get physically sick when he changed the bandages. After more than twenty years in Hartley, my parents were retiring to a house on the lake. Dad wanted to postpone the move, but Mom wouldn't hear of it. She came home from Sioux City every night and cooked, cleaned, then packed boxes until she fell asleep, dead tired. In the middle of radiation treatment, she organized an auction to sell off most of the possessions she and Dad had gathered in a lifetime. The auction took two days, and Mom was there to say good-bye to every last spoon.

Mom raised me to have that kind of strength. She knew there were no promises in life. Even when things went well, they never went easy. Mom raised six children, and she didn't have a bathroom in the house or running water until the fifth one, my sister, Val. She had boundless energy but limited time. She had chores, meals to cook, a house full of children, her chicken and egg business, and an entire community of local kids who thought of her as their mother. Mom never turned anyone away. If a child needed a meal, he'd sit with us at our table. If a family was struggling and she knew their little one liked peanut butter, the jar of peanut butter would disappear from our pantry. She had room in her heart for everyone, which didn't leave much time for any one person. Most of the time I spent with Mom growing up, I was working beside her. I was her alter ego, her other half, which was both a treasure and a burden. When Val arrived at the house after Steven's death, Mom and Dad ran out to hug her, and they all cried together. When I arrived, Dad hugged me and cried. Mom hugged me and said, 'Don't you cry. You have to be strong.' Mom knew if I was strong, she could be, too. And I knew what was expected of me.

Mom said she loved me all the time. There was never any doubt about that. Dad was the sentimental one; Mom showed her love through pride. She cried at my college graduation when she saw my summa cum laude sash. She was that proud of me for kicking off the shackles, standing up, and walking. That was her adult daughter up there, and in a way, that was her up there, too. A college graduate. With honors.

Dad couldn't attend my graduation because he was working, so my parents threw a graduation party for two hundred people back in Hartley. Dad had worked for a month to make me an apron out of a hundred one-dollar bills. One hundred dollars was a huge amount of money for my parents. In those days you were considered rich if you had two five-dollar bills to rub together. I loved that apron. It represented Dad's love and pride, just like Mom's tears. But I was so poor, it lasted only a week before I took it apart and spent it.

When my mother rallied from leukemia, no one was surprised. She had survived breast cancer five times, after all, and she was a fighter. She was on radiation treatments for years, but they never broke her. When radiation stopped working, she switched to IGG, in which parts of someone else's immune system are injected into your body. She'd have good periods, but eventually it became clear she wasn't going to win this time. She was almost eighty years old, and her strength was running out.

Mom wanted a huge party for her wedding anniversary, which was still months away. The biggest parties of our lives were for Mom and Dad's anniversaries. We four remaining children put our heads together. We didn't think Mom was going to make it to her anniversary, and besides, in her condition a huge party was out of the question. We decided to throw a small party for Mom's seventy-ninth birthday, which was only three days before Dad's eightieth birthday, just the family and a few close friends. The Jipson Family Band got together one last time and played 'Johnny M'Go.' All the children wrote poems in honor of Mom and Dad. Poems are a Jipson family tradition. Dad wrote poetry at the drop of a hat. We made fun of him for it, but we kept his poems framed on our walls or buried in our drawers, always within arm's reach.

The children agreed the poems would be silly. Here's the poem I wrote for Dad. It refers all the way back to the time I broke my engagement just out of high school.

MEMORIES OF DAD

I had broken my engagement,
John and I would never marry.
It was the hardest thing I'd every done,
Emotional and scary.

Mom was quite upset,
What would the neighbors say?
I shut myself up in my room
To cry the pain away.

Dad could hear my sobs;
This was the solace he gave:
Leaning on my doorknob, he said,
'Honey, do you want to come and watch me shave?'

But I couldn't write a silly poem for Mom. She had
done too much for me; there was too much to say.
Would I get another chance? I broke down and wrote
the kind of poem Dad was famous for, the awkwardly
sentimental kind.

MEMORIES OF MOM

When I began to pick a memory,
One day, one incident, one chat,
I realized my fondest memory
Had more substance than that.

The 70s lost my marriage – lost everything,
I could feel my life unwind.
I was depressed and struggling,
Quite literally losing my mind.

Friends and family got me through,
But with a daughter under five,
Jodi paid for all my pain
As I struggled to survive.

Thank God for Mom.
Her strength showed I could recover,
But her most important role
Back then was Jodi's second mother.

When I had no more to give,
When I fought to get out of bed,
Mom took Jodi in her arms
And kept her soul fed.

Unconditional love and stability
In that Hartley home;
Swimming lessons, silly games,
Jodi didn't have to be alone.

While I built my life back,
Studied, worked, and found my way,
Mom gave Jodi what I missed,
Special attention every day.

I was a mess while raising Jodi,
But when she fell, you caught her.
So, thank you, Mom, most of all
For helping shape our daughter.

Two days after the party, Mom woke Dad in the middle of the night and told him to drive her to the hospital. She couldn't take the pain anymore. A few days later, after she had been stabilized and sent to Sioux City for tests, we discovered Mom had colorectal cancer. Her only chance for survival, and it was no guarantee, was to remove almost her entire colon. She'd have to spend the rest of her life with a colostomy bag.

Mom had known something was seriously wrong. We found out later she had been taking suppositories and laxatives for more than a year, and she had been in almost constant pain. She hadn't wanted anyone to know. For the first time in her life, Mom didn't want to face down her enemy. She said, 'I'm not going to have the surgery. I'm tired of fighting.'

My sister was distraught. I told her, 'Val, this is Mom. Give her time.'

Sure enough, five days later Mom said, 'I don't want to go this way. Let's have the surgery.'

Mom survived the surgery and lived another eight months. They were not easy months. We brought Mom home, and Val and Dad took care of her around the clock. Val was the only one who learned to manage the colostomy bag; even the nurse couldn't change it as well. I came over every night and cooked dinner for them. Difficult times, but also some of the best of my life. Mom and I talked about everything. There was nothing left unsaid. There was no laugh we didn't share. She slipped into a coma near the end, but even then I knew she heard me. She heard all of us. She was never too far away. She died as she had lived, on her own terms, with her family at her side.

In the summer of 2006, a few months after she died, I placed a small statue outside the window of the children's library in my mother's honor. The statue is of a woman holding a book, ready to read to the child clamoring around her. To me, that statue is Mom. She always had something to give.

24

Dewey's Diet

D ad says Max II, his beloved Himalayan, will outlive him. He finds comfort in that certainty. But for most of us, living with an animal means understanding we will experience our pet's death. Animals are not children; rarely do they outlive us.

I had been mentally preparing for Dewey's death since he was fourteen years old. His colon condition and public living arrangement, according to Dr. Esterly, made it unlikely Dewey would live longer than a dozen years. But Dewey had a rare combination of genetics and attitude. By the time Dewey was seventeen, I had nearly stopped thinking about his death. I accepted it not so much as inevitable but as another milestone down the road. Since I didn't know the location of the marker, or what it would look like when we got there, why spend time worrying about it? That is to say, I enjoyed our days together, and during our evenings apart I looked no further than the next morning.

I realized Dewey was losing his hearing when he stopped responding to the word *bath*. For years, that word had sent him into a scamper. The staff would be talking, and someone would say, 'I had to clean my bathtub last night.'

Bam, Dewey was gone. Every time.

'That isn't about you, Dewey!'

But he wasn't listening. Say the word *bath* – or *brush* or *comb* or *scissors* or *doctor* or *vet* – and Dewey disappeared. Especially if Kay or I said the dread word. When I was away on library business or out sick, as I often was with my immune system so compromised by surgeries, Kay took care of Dewey. If he needed something, even comfort or love, and I wasn't around, he went to Kay. She may have been distant at first, but after all those years she had become his second mother, the one who loved him but wouldn't tolerate his bad habits. If Kay and I were standing together and even thought the word *water*, Dewey ran.

Then one day someone said *bath* and he didn't run. He still ran when I *thought* bath, but not at the word. So I started to watch him more closely. Sure enough, he had stopped running away every time a truck rumbled by in the alley behind the library. The sound of the back door opening used to send him sprinting to sniff the incoming boxes; now, he wasn't moving at all. He wasn't jumping at sudden loud noises, such as someone setting down a large reference volume too fast, and he wasn't coming as often when patrons called.

That, however, might not have had much to do with hearing. When you get older, the simple things are suddenly not so simple. A touch of arthritis, discomfort in the muscles. You thin out and stiffen up. In both cats and humans, the skin gets less elastic, which means more flaking and irritation and less ability to heal. These are not small things when your job is, essentially, to be petted all day.

Dewey still greeted everyone at the front door. He still searched out laps, but on his own terms. He had arthritis in his back left hip, and jostling him in the wrong place or picking him up the wrong way would cause him to limp away in pain. More and more in the late morning and afternoon he sat on the circulation desk, where he was protected by staff. He was supremely confident in his beauty and popularity; he knew patrons would come to him. He looked so regal, a lion surveying his kingdom. He even sat like a lion, with his paws crossed in front of him and his back legs tucked underneath, a model of dignity and grace.

The staff started quietly suggesting that patrons be gentle with Dewey, more aware of his comfort. Joy, who spent the most time out front with the patrons, became very protective of him. She often brought her nieces and nephews to see Dewey, even on her days off, so she knew how rough people could be. 'These days,' she would tell the patrons, 'Dewey prefers a gentle pat on the head.'

Even the elementary school children understood Dewey was an old man now, and they were sensitive to his needs. This was his second generation of Spencer children, the children of the children Dewey had gotten to know as a kitten, so the parents made sure their kids were well behaved. When the children touched him gently, Dewey would lie against their legs or, if they were sitting on the floor, on their laps. But he was more cautious than he used to be, and loud noise or rough petting often drove him away.

'That's all right, Dewey. Whatever you need.'

After years of trial and error, we had finally found our finicky cat an acceptable cat bed. It was small, with white fake fur sides and an electric warmer in the bottom. We kept it in front of the wall heater outside my office door. Dewey loved nothing more than lounging in his bed, in the safety of the staff area, with the heating pad turned all the way up. In the winter, when the wall heater was on, he got so warm he had to throw himself over the side and roll around on the floor. His fur was so hot you couldn't even touch it. He would lie on his back for ten minutes with all his legs spread out, venting heat. If a cat could pant, Dewey would have been panting. As soon as he was cool, he climbed back into his bed and started the process all over again.

Heat wasn't Dewey's only indulgence. I may have been a sucker for Dewey's whims, but now our assistant children's librarian, Donna, was spoiling him even more than I did. If Dewey didn't eat his food right away, she heated it in the microwave for him. If he still didn't eat it, she threw it out and opened another can. Donna didn't trust ordinary flavors. Why should Dewey eat gizzards and toes? Donna drove to Milford, fifteen miles away, because a little store there sold exotic cat food. I remember duck. Dewey was fond of that for a week. She tried lamb, too, but as usual nothing stuck for very long. Donna kept trying new flavor after new flavor and new can after new can. Oh, how she loved that cat.

Despite our best efforts, though, Dewey was thinning down, so at his next checkup Dr. Franck prescribed a series of medicines to fatten him up. That's right, despite the dire health warnings, Dewey had outlasted his old nemesis, Dr. Esterly, who retired at the end of 2002 and donated his practice to a nonprofit animal advocacy group.

Along with the pills, Dr. Franck gave me a pill shooter which, theoretically, shot the pills far enough down Dewey's throat that he couldn't spit them out. But Dewey was smart. He took his pill so calmly I thought, 'Good, we made it. That was easy.' That's when he snuck behind a shelf somewhere and coughed it back up. I found little white pills all over the library.

I didn't force Dewey's medicine on him. He was eighteen; if he didn't want medicine, he didn't have to take it. Instead, I bought him a container of yogurt and started giving him a lick every day. That opened the floodgates. Kay started giving him bites of cold cuts out of her sandwiches. Joy started sharing her ham sandwich, and pretty soon Dewey was following her to the kitchen whenever he saw her walk through the door with a bag in her hand. One day Sharon left a sandwich unwrapped on her desk. When she came back a minute later, the top slice of bread had been carefully turned over and placed to the side. The bottom slice of bread was sitting exactly where it had been, untouched. But all the meat was gone.

After Thanksgiving of 2005, we discovered Dewey loved turkey, so the staff loaded up on holiday scraps. We tried to freeze them, but he could always tell when the turkey wasn't fresh. Dewey never lost his keen sense of smell. That's one reason I scoffed when Sharon offered Dewey a bite of garlic chicken, her favorite microwavable lunch. I told her, 'No way Dewey is going to eat garlic.'

He ate every bite. Who was this cat? For eighteen years, Dewey ate nothing but specific brands and flavors of cat food. Now, it seemed, he'd eat anything.

I thought, 'If we can fatten Dewey up on human food, why not? Isn't that better than a pill?'

I bought him braunschweiger, a cold loaf of sliced liver sausage many people around here consider a delicacy. Braunschweiger is about 80 percent pure fat. If anything would fatten Dewey up, it was braunschweiger. He wouldn't touch it.

What Dewey really wanted, we discovered accidentally, was Arby's Beef 'n Cheddar sandwiches. He gobbled them down. Inhaled them. He didn't even chew the beef; he just sucked it in. I don't know what was in those sandwiches, but once he started on Arby's Beef 'n Cheddar, Dewey's digestion improved. His constipation decreased dramatically. He started eating two cans of cat food a day, and because the fast food was so salty, he was slurping down a full dish of water as well. He even started using the litter box on his own.

But Dewey didn't have a couple owners, he had hundreds, and most of them couldn't see the improvements. All they saw was the cat they loved getting thinner and thinner. Dewey never hesitated to play up his condition. He would sit on the circulation desk and whenever someone approached to pet him, he would whine. They always fell for it.

'What's the matter, Dewey?'

He led them to the entrance to the staff area, where they could see his food dish. He'd look forlornly at the food, then back at them, and with his big eyes full of sorrow, drop his head.

'Vicki! Dewey's hungry!'

'He has a can of food in the bowl.'

'But he doesn't like it.'

'That's his second flavor this morning. I threw the first can away an hour ago.'

'But he's crying. Look at him. He just flopped down on the floor.'

'We can't just give him cans of food all day.'

'What about something else?'

'He ate an Arby's sandwich this morning.'

'Look at him. He's so thin. You guys have to be feed him more.'

'We're taking good care of him.'

'But he's so thin. Can't you give him something for me?'

I could, except Dewey did the same thing yesterday. And the day before that. And the day before that. In fact, you're the fifth person he's hit with the starving-cat routine today.

Now, how was I going to tell a patron that? I always gave in, which of course just encouraged more bad behavior. I think Dewey enjoyed the taste of food more when he knew I didn't want to give it to him. Let's call it the taste of victory.

25

The Meeting

As Dewey entered old age, the kindness of Spencer Public Library patrons really began to show. Friends and visitors alike were gentler around him. They talked to him more and were attentive to his needs, much as you would be to an older relative at a family reunion. Occasionally someone would comment that he looked weak, or thin, or dirty, but I knew their concern was a manifestation of their love.

'What's wrong with his fur?' was probably the most common question.

'Nothing,' I told them. 'He's just old.'

It's true, Dewey's fur had lost much of its luster.

It was no longer radiant orange, but a dull copper. It was also increasingly matted, so much so I couldn't keep up with a simple brushing. I took Dewey to Dr. Franck, who explained that as cats aged, the barbs on their tongues wore down. Even if they licked themselves regularly, they couldn't do an efficient job grooming because there was nothing to separate the fur. Tangles and mats were just another symptom of old age.

'As for these,' Dr. Franck said, studying Dewey's clumped back end, 'drastic measures are required. I think we better shave.'

When she was done, poor Dewey was fuzzy on one end, bare on the other. He looked like he was wearing a big mink coat and no pants. A few members of the staff laughed when they saw him, because it was a hilarious sight, but they didn't laugh long. The humiliation on Dewey's face stopped that. He hated it. Just hated it. He walked away very fast for a few steps, then sat down and tried to hide his rear end. Then he got up, walked quickly away, and sat down again. Start, stop. Start, stop. He finally made it back to his bed, buried his head in his paws, and curled up beneath his favorite toy, Marty Mouse. For days, we found him with his top half sticking out into an aisle and his back end hidden in a bookshelf.

But Dewey's health was no laughing matter. The staff didn't talk about it, but I knew they were worried. They were afraid they would come in one morning and find Dewey dead on the floor. It wasn't his death that worried some of them, I realized, but the thought of having to deal with it themselves. Or even worse, having to make a decision in a health crisis. Between my own health issues and my trips to Des Moines on state library business, I was frequently out of the library. Dewey was my cat, and everyone knew it. The last thing they wanted was to have the life of my cat in their hands.

'Don't worry,' I told them. 'Just do what you think is best for Dewey. You can't do anything wrong.'

I couldn't promise the staff nothing would happen while I was away, but I told them, 'I know this cat. I know when he is healthy, a little sick, and really sick. If he's really sick, trust me, he's going to the vet. I'll do whatever it takes.'

Besides, Dewey wasn't sick. He still jumped up and down from the circulation desk, so I knew his arthritis wasn't too bad. His digestion was better than ever. And he still loved the company of patrons. But it took patience to care for an elderly cat, and frankly, some of the staff didn't think that was their job. Slowly, as Dewey aged, his support peeled away: first those in town with different agendas; then some of the fence-sitters; then a few patrons who wanted only an attractive, active cat; and finally the staff members who didn't want the burden of geriatric care.

That doesn't mean I wasn't blindsided by the October 2006 library board meeting. I was expecting a typical discussion of the state of the library, but the meeting soon turned into a referendum on Dewey. A patron had mentioned he wasn't looking well. Perhaps, the board suggested, we should get him some medical help?

'At his recent checkup,' I told them, 'Dr. Franck discovered hyperthyroidism. It's just another symptom of age, like his arthritis, his dry skin, and the black age spots on his lips and gums. Dr. Franck prescribed a medication that, thank goodness, doesn't have to be taken orally. I rub it in his ear. Dewey has really perked up. And don't worry,' I reminded them, 'we're paying for the medicine with donations and my own money. Not a single penny of city money is ever spent on Dewey's care.'

'Is hyperthyroidism serious?'

'Yes, but it's treatable.'

'Will this medicine help his fur?'

'Dullness isn't a disease, it's a function of age, like gray hair on a human.' They should understand. There wasn't a head in the room without a few gray hairs.

'What about his weight?'

I explained his diet in detail, from the obsessiveness with which Donna and I changed his cat food to the Arby's Beef 'n Cheddar sandwiches.

'But he doesn't look good.'

They kept coming back to that. Dewey didn't look good. Dewey was hurting the image of the library. I knew they meant well, that they were interested in finding the best solution for everyone, but I couldn't understand their thinking. It was true, Dewey didn't look as appealing. Everybody ages. Eighty-year-olds don't look like twenty-year-olds, and they shouldn't. We live in a throwaway culture that stashes older people away and tries not to look at them. They have wrinkles. They have age spots. They don't walk well and their hands shake. Their eyes are watery, or they drool when they eat, or they 'burp in their pants' too much (Jodi's phrase from when she was two years old). We don't want to see that. Even the accomplished elderly, even the people who gave their whole lives, we want them out of sight and out of mind. But maybe older people, and old cats, have something to teach us, if not about the world, then about ourselves.

'Why don't you take Dewey home to live with you? I know he visits you on holidays.'

I had thought of that but dismissed it long ago. Dewey could never be happy living at my house. I was gone too much, between work and meetings. He hated to be alone. He was a public cat. He needed people around him, he needed the library around him, to be happy.

'We've had complaints, Vicki, don't you understand? Our job is to speak for the citizens of this town.'

The board seemed ready to say the town didn't want Dewey anymore. I knew that was ridiculous because I saw the community's love for Dewey every day. I had no doubt the board had received a few complaints, but there had always been complaints. Now, with Dewey not looking his best, the voices were louder. But that didn't mean the town had turned on Dewey. One thing I'd learned over the years was that the people who loved Dewey, who really wanted and needed him, weren't the ones with the loudest voices. They were often the ones with no voices at all.

If this had been the board twenty years ago, I realized, we would never have been able to adopt Dewey. 'Thank God,' I thought to myself. 'Thank you, God, for past boards.'

And even if what the board thought was true, even if the majority of the town had turned its back on Dewey, didn't we nonetheless have the duty to stand by him? Even if five people cared, wasn't that enough? Even if nobody cared, the fact remained that Dewey loved the town of Spencer. He would always love Spencer. He needed us. We couldn't just toss him out because looking at him, older and weaker, no longer made us proud.

There was another message from the board, too, and it came through loud and clear: Dewey is not your cat. He's the town's cat. We speak for the town, so it's our decision. We know what's best.

I won't argue one fact. Dewey was Spencer's cat. Nothing has ever been truer. But he was also my cat. And finally, in the end, Dewey was *a* cat. At that meeting, I realized that in many people's minds, Dewey had gone from being a flesh-and-blood animal with thoughts and feelings, to being a symbol, a metaphor, an object that could be owned. Library board members loved Dewey as a cat – Kathy Greiner, the president, always carried treats in her pocket for Dewey – but they still couldn't separate the animal from the legacy.

And I have to admit, there was another thought going through my mind. 'I'm getting older, too. My health isn't the best. Are these people going to throw me out on my ear, too?'

'I know I am close to Dewey,' I told the board. 'I know I've been through a hard year with the death of my mother and with my health, and that you're trying to protect me. But I don't need protecting.' I stopped. That wasn't what I was trying to say at all.

'Maybe you think I love Dewey too much,' I told them. 'Maybe you think my love clouds my judgment. But trust me. I'll know when it's time. I've had animals all my life. I've put them down. It's hard, but I can do it. The very last thing I want, the very last thing, is for Dewey to suffer.'

A board meeting can be a freight train, and this one pushed me off to the side like a cow on the tracks. Someone suggested a committee to make decisions about Dewey's future. I knew the people on that committee would mean well. I knew they would take their duty seriously and do what they thought best. But I couldn't let that happen. I just couldn't.

The board was discussing how many people should be on this Dewey Death Watch Committee when one member, Sue Hitchcock, spoke up. 'This is ridiculous,' she said. 'I can't believe we're even discussing this. Vicki has been at the library for twenty-five years. She's been with Dewey for nineteen years. She knows what she's doing. We should all trust Vicki's judgment.'

Thank God for Sue Hitchcock. As soon as she spoke, the train jumped the tracks and the board backed off. 'Yes, yes,' they muttered, 'you're right . . . too soon, too much . . . if his condition worsens . . .'

I was devastated. It stung me to the heart that these people had even suggested taking Dewey away from me. And they could have done it. They had the power. But they didn't. Somehow, we had won a victory: for Dewey, for the library, for the town. For me.

26

Dewey's Love

I'll always remember Christmas 2005, the year before that horrible meeting, when Dewey was eighteen. Jodi and Scott stayed at my house. They had twins now, Nathan and Hannah, a year and a half old. Mom was still alive, and she put on her best lounging outfit to watch the twins open presents. Dewey sprawled on the sofa, pressed against Jodi's hip. It was the end of one thing, the beginning of the next. But for that week, we were all together.

Dewey's love for Jodi had never diminished. She was still his great romantic affair. Whenever he got a chance that Christmas, Dewey stuck by her side. But with so many people around, especially the children, and with so much going on, he was more content than ever to just watch. He got along well with Scott, not a hint of jealousy. And he loved the twins. I replaced my glass coffee table with a cushioned ottoman when my grandchildren were born, and Dewey spent most of Christmas week sitting on that ottoman. Hannah and Nathan would toddle up and pet him all over. Dewey was cautious around toddlers now. In the library, he slunk away when they tried to approach him. But he sat with the twins, even when they petted him the wrong way and messed up his fur. Hannah kissed him a hundred times a day; Nathan accidentally knocked him on the head. One afternoon, Hannah poked Dewey in the face while trying to pet him. Dewey didn't even react. This was my grandchild, Jodi's child. Dewey loved us, so he loved Hannah, too.

Dewey was so calm that year. That was the biggest difference in old man Dewey. He knew how to avoid trouble. He still attended meetings, but he knew how far to push and which lap to choose. In September 2006, just a few weeks before the board meeting, a program at the library brought in almost a hundred people. I figured Dewey would hide in the staff area, but there he was, mingling as always. He was like a shadow moving among the guests, often unnoticed but somehow there at the end of a patron's hand each time someone reached to pet him. There was a rhythm to his interactions that seemed the most natural and beautiful thing in the world.

After the program, Dewey climbed into his bed above Kay's desk, clearly exhausted. Kay came over and gave him a gentle scratch on the chin. I knew that touch, that quiet look. It was a thank-you, the one you give an old friend or a spouse after you've watched them across a crowded room and realized how wonderful they are, and how lucky you are to have them in your life. I half expected her to say, 'That'll do, cat, that'll do,' like the farmer in the movie *Babe*, but this time Kay left all the words unsaid.

Two months later, in early November, Dewey's gait became a bit unsteady. He started peeing excessively, sometimes on the paper outside his litter box, which he had never done before. But he wasn't hiding. He was still jumping up and down from the circulation desk. He still interacted with patrons. He didn't seem to be in pain. I called Dr. Franck, and she advised me not to bring him in but to watch him closely.

One morning near the end of the month, Dewey wasn't waving. All those years, and I could count on one hand the number of times Dewey wasn't waving when I arrived in the morning. Instead he was standing at the front door, just waiting for me. I ushered him to the litter box and gave him his can of cat food. He ate a few bites, then walked with me on our morning rounds. I was busy preparing for a trip to Florida – my brother Mike's daughter Natalie was getting married and the whole family was going to be there – so I left Dewey with the staff for the rest of the morning. As always, he came in while I was working to sniff my office vent and make sure I was safe. The older he got, the more he protected the ones he loved.

At nine thirty I went out for Dewey's breakfast of the moment, a Hardee's bacon, egg, and cheese biscuit. When I returned, Dewey didn't come running. I figured the deaf old boy didn't hear the door. I found him sleeping on a chair by the circulation desk, so I swung the bag a few times, floating the smell of eggs his way. He flew out of that chair into my office. I put the egg-and-cheese mush on a paper plate, and he ate three or four bites before curling up on my lap.

At ten thirty, Dewey attended Story Hour. As usual, he greeted every child. An eight-year-old girl was sitting on the floor with her legs crossed, in the position we used to call Indian-style. Dewey curled up on her legs and went to sleep. She petted him, the other children took turns petting him, everyone was happy. After Story Hour, Dewey crawled into his fur-lined bed in front of the heater, which was running full blast, and that's where he was when I left the library at noon. I was going home for lunch, then picking up Dad and driving to Omaha to catch a flight the next morning.

Ten minutes after I got home, the phone rang. It was Jann, one of our clerks. 'Dewey's acting funny.'

'What do you mean funny?'

'He's crying and walking funny. And he's trying to hide in the cupboards.'

'I'll be right down.'

Dewey was hiding under a chair. I picked him up, and he was shaking like the morning I found him. His eyes were big, and I could tell he was in pain. I called the veterinary office. Dr. Franck was out, but her husband, Dr. Beall, was in. He said, 'Come right down.' I wrapped Dewey in his towel. It was a cold day, the end of November. Dewey snuggled against me immediately.

By the time we arrived at the vet's office, Dewey was down on the floor of my car by the heater, shaking with fear. I cradled him in my arms and held him against my chest. That's when I noticed poop sticking out of his behind.

What a relief! It wasn't serious. It was constipation.

I told Dr. Beall the problem. He took Dewey into the back room to clean out his colon and intestines. He also washed his back end, so Dewey came back wet and cold. He crawled from Dr. Beall's arms into mine and looked up at me with pleading eyes. *Help me*. I could tell something still wasn't right.

Dr. Beall said, 'I can feel a mass. It's not feces.'

'What is it?'

'He needs an X-ray.'

Ten minutes later, Dr. Beall was back with the results. There was a large tumor in Dewey's stomach, and it was pushing on his kidneys and intestines. That's why he had been peeing more, and it probably accounted for his peeing outside the litter box.

'It wasn't there in September,' Dr. Beall said, 'which means it's probably an aggressive cancer. But we'd have to do invasive tests to find out for sure.'

We stood silently, looking at Dewey. I never suspected the tumor. Never. I knew everything about Dewey, all his thoughts and feelings, but he had kept this one thing hidden from me.

'Is he in pain?'

'Yes, I suspect he is. The mass is growing very fast, so it will only get worse.'

'Is there anything you can give him for the pain?'

'No, not really.'

I was holding Dewey in my arms, cradling him like a baby. He hadn't let me carry him that way in sixteen years. Now he wasn't even fighting it. He was just looking at me.

'Do you think he's in constant pain?'

'I can't imagine that he's not.'

The conversation was crushing me, flattening me out, making me feel drawn, deflated, tired. I couldn't believe what I was hearing. Somehow I had believed Dewey was going to live forever.

I called the library staff and told them Dewey wasn't coming home. Kay was out of town. Joy was off duty. They reached her at Sears, but too late. Several others came down to say their good-byes. Instead of going to Dewey, though, Sharon walked right up and hugged me. Thank you, Sharon, I needed that. Then I hugged Donna and thanked her for loving Dewey so much. Donna was the last to say her good-byes.

Someone said, 'I don't know if I want to be here when they put him to sleep.'

'That's fine,' I said. 'I'd rather be alone with him.'

Dr. Beall took Dewey into the back room to insert the IV, then brought him back in a fresh blanket and put him in my arms. I talked to Dewey for a few minutes. I told him how much I loved him, how much he meant to me, how much I didn't want him to suffer. I explained what was happening and why. I rewrapped his blanket to make sure he was comfortable. What more could I offer him than comfort? I cradled him in my arms and rocked back and forth from foot to foot, a habit started when he was a kitten. Dr. Beall gave him the first shot, followed closely by the second.

He said, 'I'll check for a heartbeat.'

I said, 'You don't need to. I can see it in his eyes.'

Dewey was gone.

27

Loving Dewey

I was in Florida for eight days. I didn't read the newspaper. I didn't watch television. I didn't take any phone calls. It was the best possible time to be away because Dewey's death was hard. Very hard. I broke down on the flight from Omaha and cried all the way to Houston. In Florida, I thought often of Dewey, alone, quietly, but also surrounded by the family that had always sustained me.

I had no idea how far word of Dewey's death had spread. The next morning, while I sat crying on an airplane to Houston, the local radio station devoted their morning show to memories of Dewey. The

Sioux City Journal ran a lengthy story and obituary. I don't know if that was the source, but the AP wire picked up the story and sent it around the world. Within hours, news of Dewey's death appeared on the CBS afternoon newsbreak and on MSNBC. The library started getting calls. If I had been in the library, I would have been stuck answering questions from reporters for days, but nobody else on staff felt comfortable speaking to the media. The library secretary, Kim, gave a brief statement, which ended up in what I now think of as Dewey's public obituary, but that was all. It was enough. Over the next few days, that obituary ran in more than 270 newspapers.

The response from individuals touched by Dewey was equally overwhelming. People in town received calls from friends and relatives all over the country who read about Dewey's death in the local newspaper or heard it on a local radio show. One local couple was out of the country and learned the news from a friend in San Francisco, who read about his passing in the *San Francisco Chronicle*. Admirers set up a vigil in the library. Local businesses sent flowers and gifts. Sharon and Tony's daughter, Emmy, gave me a picture she had drawn of Dewey. It was two green circles in the middle of the page with lines sticking out in all directions. It was beautiful, and Emmy beamed as I taped it to my office door. That picture was the perfect way for both of us to remember him.

Gary Roma, director of the documentary about library cats, wrote me a long letter. It said, in part:

'I don't know if I ever told you, but of all the many library cats I've met across the country, Dewey Readmore Books was my favorite. His beauty, charm, and playfulness were unique.'

Tomoko from Japanese Public Television wrote to tell us Dewey's death had been announced in Japan, and that many were sad to hear he was gone.

Marti Attoun, who wrote the article for *American Profile*, wrote to say the Dewey story was still her favorite. It had been years, and Marti was now a contributing editor. It seemed so unlikely, given the hundreds of stories she had written, that Marti would remember a cat, much less still think of him fondly. But that was Dewey. He touched people so deeply.

By the time I returned to my office, there were letters and cards stacked four feet high on my desk. I had more than six hundred e-mails about Dewey waiting in my inbox. Many were from people who met him only once but never forgot him. Hundreds of others were from people who never met him. In the month after his death, I received more than a thousand e-mails about Dewey from all around the world. We heard from a soldier in Iraq who had been touched by Dewey's death despite what he saw there every day – or perhaps because of it. We received a letter from a couple in Connecticut whose son was turning eleven; his birthday wish was to release a balloon to heaven in Dewey's honor. We received numerous gifts and donations. A librarian at the Naval History Museum, for instance, donated four books in his memory. She had followed Dewey's story in library publications and read his obituary in the *Washington Post*. Our Web site, www.spencerlibrary. com, went from 25,000 hits a month to 189,922 in December, and the traffic didn't let up for most of the next year.

Many people in town wanted us to hold a memorial service. I didn't want a memorial service, nobody on staff did, but we had to do something. So on a cold Saturday in the middle of December, Dewey's admirers gathered at the library to remember one last time, at least officially, the friend who had had such an impact on their lives. The staff tried to keep it light – I told the story of the bat, Audrey told the story of the lights, Joy remembered the cart rides, Sharon told how Dewey stole the meat out of her sandwich – but despite our best efforts, tears were shed. Two women cried the whole time.

Crews from local television stations were filming the event. It was a nice thought, but the cameras seemed out of place. These were private thoughts among friends; we didn't want to share our words with the world. We also realized, as we stood there together, that words couldn't describe our feelings for Dewey. There was no easy way to say how special he was. We were here; the cameras were here; the world stood still around us. That said more than any words. Finally a local schoolteacher said, 'People say what's the big deal, he was just a cat. But that's where they're wrong. Dewey was so much more.' Everyone knew exactly what she meant.

My moments with Dewey were more intimate. The staff had cleaned out his bowls and donated his food while I was away, but I had to give away his toys. I had to clean out his shelf: the Vaseline for his hairballs, the brush, the red skein of yarn he had played with all his life. I had to park my car and walk to the library every morning without Dewey waving at me from the front door. When the staff returned to the library after visiting Dewey for the last time, the space heater he had lain in front of every day wasn't working. Dewey had been lying in front of it that very morning, and it had been working fine. It was as if his death had taken away its reason to heat. Can a malfunctioning piece of equipment break your heart? It was six weeks before I could even think about having that heater repaired.

I had Dewey cremated with one of his favorite toys, Marty Mouse, so he wouldn't be alone. The crematorium offered a mahogany box and bronze plaque, no charge, but it didn't seem right to display him. Dewey came back to his library in a plain plastic container inside a blue velvet bag. I put the container on a shelf in my office and went back to work.

A week after his memorial service, I came out of my office a half hour before the library opened, long before any patrons arrived, and told Kay, 'It's time.'

It was December, another brutally cold Iowa morning. Just like the first morning, and so many in between. It was close to the shortest day of the year, and the sun wasn't yet up. The sky was still deep blue, almost purple, and there was no traffic on the roads.

The only sound was the cold wind that had come all the way from the Canadian plains, whipping down the streets and out over the barren cornfields.

We moved some rocks in the little garden out front of the library, looking for a place where the ground wasn't completely frozen. But the whole earth was frosted, and it took a while for Kay to dig the hole. The sun was peeking over the buildings on the far side of the parking lot, throwing the first shadows, by the time I placed the remains of my friend in the ground and said simply, 'You're always with us, Dewey. This is your home.' Then Kay dropped in the first shovelful of dirt, burying Dewey's ashes forever outside the window of the children's library, at the foot of the beautiful statue of a mother reading a book to her child. Mom's statue. As Kay moved the stones back over Dewey's final resting place, I looked up and saw the rest of the library staff in the window, silently watching us.

EPILOGUE

Last Thoughts from Iowa

Not much has changed in northwest Iowa since Dewey died. With ethanol being the next big thing, more corn is in the ground than ever before, but there aren't more workers to grow it, just better technology and more machines. And, of course, more land.

In Spencer, the hospital added its first plastic surgeon. Cleber Meyer, now eighty, was voted out of office and went back to his gas station. The new mayor is the husband of Kim Petersen, the library secretary, but he's no more a reader than Cleber was. The Eaton plant on the edge of town, which makes machine parts, moved a shift to Juárez, Mexico. One hundred and twenty jobs lost. But Spencer will survive. We always do.

The library rolls on, cat-free for the first time since Ronald Reagan was president. After Dewey's death, we had almost a hundred offers for new cats. We had offers from as far away as Texas, transportation included. The cats were cute, and most had touching survival stories, but there was no enthusiasm to take one. The library board wisely put a two-year moratorium on cats in the library. They needed time, they said, to think through the issues. I had done all the thinking I needed. You can't bring back the past.

But Dewey's memory will live on, I feel confident of that. Maybe at the library, where his portrait hangs beside the front door above a bronze plaque that tells his story, a gift from one of Dewey's many friends. Maybe in the children who knew him, who will talk about him in decades to come with their own children and grandchildren. Maybe in this book. After all, that's why I'm writing it. For Dewey.

Back in 2000, when Grand Avenue made the National Registry, Spencer commissioned a public art installation to serve as both a statement about our values and an entry point to our historic downtown. Two Chicago-area ceramic tile mosaic artists, Nina Smoot-Cain and John Pitman Weber, spent a year in the area, talking with us, studying our history, and observing our way of life. More than 570 residents, from young children to grandparents, consulted with the artists. The result is a mosaic sculpture called *The Gathering: Of Time, of Land, of Many Hands*.

The Gathering is composed of four decorative pillars and three pictorial walls. The south wall is called 'The Story of the Land.' It is a farm scene featuring corn and pigs; a woman hanging quilts on a clothesline; and a train. The north wall is 'The Story of Outdoor Recreation.' It focuses on East and West Lynch parks, our main municipal recreation areas; the fairgrounds on the northwest edge of town; and the lakes. The west wall is 'The Story of Spencer.'

It shows three generations gathering at grandma's house; the town battling the fire; and a woman making a pot, a metaphor for shaping the future. Just slightly to the left of center, in the upper half of the scene, is an orange cat sitting on the open pages of a book. The image is based on artwork submitted by a child.

The story of Spencer. Dewey is a part of it, then, now, and forever. He will live longest, I know, in the collective memory of a town that never forgets where it's been, even as it looks ahead for where it's going.

I told Jodi when Dewey was fourteen, 'I don't know if I'll want to keep working at the library after Dewey's gone.' It was just a premonition, but now I understand what I meant. For as long as I can remember, when I pulled up every morning the library was alive: with hope, with love, with Dewey waving at me from the front door. Now it's a dead building again. I feel the chill in my bones, even in the summer. Some mornings, I don't want to bother. But then I turn on the lights, and the library flickers to life. The staff files in. The patrons follow: the middle-aged for books, the businessmen for magazines, the teenagers for computers, the children for stories, the elderly for support. The library is alive, and once again I have the best job on earth, at least until I get ready to leave in the evening and there's nobody begging for one more game of hide-and-seek.

A year after Dewey's death, my health finally caught up with me. It was time, I knew, to move on with my life. The library was different without Dewey, and I didn't want my days to end that way: empty, quiet, occasionally lonely. When I saw the book cart go past, the one Dewey used to ride on, it broke my heart. I missed him that much, and not just once in a while, but every day. I decided to retire. It was time. More than 125 people attended my retirement party, including many from out of town I hadn't spoken with in years. Dad read one of his poems; my grandkids sat with me to greet well-wishers; two articles ran in the *Spencer Daily Reporter* thanking me for twenty-five years of service. Like Dewey, I was lucky. I got to leave on my own terms.

Find your place. Be happy with what you have. Treat everyone well. Live a good life. It isn't about material things; it's about love. And you can never anticipate love.

I learned those things from Dewey, of course, but as always, those answers seem too easy. All answers, except that I loved Dewey with all my heart and he loved me in the same way, seem too easy. But let me try.

When I was three years old, Dad owned a John Deere tractor. The tractor had a cultivator on the front, which is a long row of shovel-like blades, six on each side. The blades are raised a few inches off the dirt; you drive the handle forward to put them in the ground, where they chop into the soil, tossing fresh dirt against the corn rows. I was playing in the mud by the front wheel of that tractor one day when Mom's brother came out after lunch, threw the clutch, and started driving. Dad saw what happened and started running, but Mom's brother couldn't hear him. The wheel knocked me down and shoved me into the blades. I was pushed along by the blades, passed from one to the other, until Mom's brother turned the wheel and the inside blade tossed me through the middle chute and left me lying facedown behind the tractor. Dad scooped me up in one motion and ran me back to the porch. He looked me over in amazement, then held me in his arms for the rest of the day, rocking back and forth in our old rocking chair, crying on my shoulder and telling me, 'You're all right, you're all right, everything is all right.'

Eventually I looked at him and said, 'I cut my finger.' I showed him the blood. I was bruised, but otherwise, that tiny cut was the only mark.

That's life. We all go through the tractor blades every now and then. We all get bruised, and we all get cut. Sometimes the blades cut deep. The lucky ones come through with a few scratches, a little blood, but even that isn't the most important thing. The most important thing is having someone there to scoop you up, to hold you tight, and to tell you everything is all right.

For years, I thought I had done that for Dewey. I thought that was my story to tell. And I had done that. When Dewey was hurt, cold, and crying, I was there. I held him. I made sure everything was all right.

But that's only a sliver of the truth. The real truth is that for all those years, on the hard days, the good days, and all the unremembered days that make up the pages of the real book of our lives, Dewey was holding me.

He's still holding me now. So thank you, Dewey. Thank you. Wherever you are.

ACKNOWLEDGMENTS

To my agent, Peter McGuigan, for contacting me and believing there was a story to be told about Dewey's life. Thank you, Peter, Hannah Gordon Brown, and everyone at Foundry Literary who worked so tirelessly to make this book bigger than I ever imagined.

To Bret Witter, who not only found my voice, but also became a friend and confidant through this process. Thank you, Bret, for making the book so well written. We were passionate about quality, and I think we achieved it.

To Karen Kosztolnyik, Jamie Raab, and Celia Johnson at Grand Central Publishing for fighting for the book even though they saw only a forty-five-page proposal. They believed in the story before it was even written. Thank you to Matthew Ballast, Harvey-Jane Kowal, Christine Valentine, and everyone at Grand Central: there would be no book without all of you.

To Dick Montgomery for being my lawyer and friend through all the legal 'stuff,' and to his wife, Mary Jean, for all her support.

To the current and former Spencer Library staff who supported this project, sat through interviews, believed in me, and cared for Dewey over the years, including Jean Hollis Clark, Kay Larson, Joy DeWall, Sharon Joy, Audrey Wheeler, Cynthia Behrends, Paula Brown, Donna Stanford, Tammi Herbold, Jann Arends, Mary Jo Wingrove, Doris Armstrong, Kari Palm, Sheryl Rose, and Jackie Webster.

To all the other folks who agreed to be interviewed for this book and filled in my memory gaps, including Bob Rose, Kirby Schmidt, Mike Baehr, Jack Manders, Cathy Greiner, Esther Connell, Judy Johnson (both of you!), Marcie Muckey, Pat Jones, Dr. James Esterly, Verlyn Jipson, and Jodi Carlson. And to Louisville Metro Transcription, for transcribing those hundreds of hours of interviews.

To the board members who were in place when the decision was made to adopt Dewey, including Jack Manders, Mike Baehr, Mary Houston, Esther Connell, Bernie Keninger, JoAnn Lawson, Gail Peterson, Lee Lookingbill, and Grace Rindsig. They made a quick decision that would affect the library for years. I always had their full support; they gave me wings to fly.

To the current board members who gave me permission to write this book (on my own time), including Cathy Greiner, Esther Connell, Jim Morony, Sue Hitchcock, Roger Littlefield, Wayne Koppen, and Amanda Hoffman.

To the Board of the Friends Group who were always there when I needed them, especially Sandy Fleck, Marcie Muckey, and Trudy Elbert.

To my family, who helped me with the book and

supported me through the process: Verlyn Jipson; Jodi and Scott Carlson; brother Doug (who edited film of Dewey), Merrillee, Verlyn, James, and Merrill Jipson; brother Mike and Monica Jipson, and daughter, Natalie DeHaven; sister Val and Don Bonney, Andrea, Josh, and Lindsay; and my niece MacKenzie Dunn. To my brothers David and Steve, whose lives were rich but much too short. To my mom and grandma Stephenson, who were strong role models for my life. And, most of all, to my delightful twin grandchildren, who make me laugh when the stress is too much: Hannah and Nathan Carlson.

To my uncle, Duane Jipson, who read everything he could get his hands on (including the encyclopedia) until his death at age ninety-four. His example of love, kindness, gentility, and education touched everyone, and especially me.

To Jim Fanning, former manager of the Montreal Expos baseball team and lifelong friend, for his support during the lean times and for believing that I could accomplish anything.

To Dr. Ron Kolegraff, friend and surgeon, for understanding my emotional needs when no one else could see it or discuss it.

To Treva Johnson, for helping me understand the needs of the disabled in the library long before the ADA Act was passed and for being my colleague on the Spencer ADA Council since 1991.

To Dewey fans, both near and far, for the thousands of letters, e-mails, gifts, and personal visits to see

Dewey over the years, especially Harry and Rita Fein, from New York (who remembered every year for Christmas), Doreen Walker (his first British pen pal), Phyllis Lahti (founder of the Library Cat Society), and Gary Roma (filmmaker and comedian), who all believed in Dewey's magic before he was famous.

To the city of Spencer staff and council who stood up for me and supported the library over the years, especially city council member David Scott, who volunteered his time as Board of the Friends attorney for over twenty-five years and went to bat for me many times. And to Bob Fagen, current city manager, who treated me with respect and understood the significance of this book for Spencer.

To my friends, who always got me through the dark times and laughed with me in the good times, including my Run Away Women friends who consulted on the book: Trudy Henry, Faith Landwer, Barb Feder, Idelle Walton, Rita Mathine, and Pauli Wright. To Bonnie McKewon, friend and colleague, who read an early manuscript and made suggestions; her husband, Ron McKewon, who supported Dewey though his art; Dorothy DeGroot; and my many local friends for keeping me sane.

To my mentor, Dr. Roger Greer, and the professors from Emporia, who gave me the knowledge and tools for a successful career, not just in Spencer but across Iowa and beyond. I still use 'Greerisms' in all the classes and workshops I teach.

To Dewey's doctors, Dr. James Esterly, Dr. Sophi

Franck, and Dr. Tom Beall, for taking gentle care of him. To 'Ashes To Ashes' for donating cremation of Dewey's remains along with his fur basket to keep him warm and Marty Mouse to keep him company. To Warner Funeral Home, thank you for donating Dewey's memorial stone.

And, finally, to Dewey, my magical little buddy for more than nineteen years. I can still feel the heartstring that connects us, and I will never let go.

Special Thanks to the great Iowa writer Bill Kinsella, whom I had long admired but never met, for his wonderful endorsement and for allowing me to paraphrase from his book *Shoeless Joe* (and the movie based on it, *Field of Dreams*) on page 142. No one will ever express the magic of Iowa any better.

Cats Protection rehomes and reunites over 55,500 cats a year creating many happy endings throughout the UK.

Not all cats are as lucky as Dewey and we have many in our care who need your help.

If you would like to support Cats Protection, please visit www.cats.org.uk/dewey or contact us at :

Cats Protection
Dewey Appeal
National Cat Centre
Chelwood Gate
Haywards Heath
RH17 7TT

www.cats.org.uk/dewey

Reg charity 203644 (England and Wales) SC037711 (Scotland)